THE
SEED

For life in the Kingdom of God

Immanuel Sun

―― *Published By* ――
NEW STREAMS STUDIO

Copyright © 2017 by Immanuel Sun. All Rights Reserved.
www.kingdomage.org

First Edition, October 2017

Edited by Cheryl Lowe

Designed by Elaine Cochran

Published in Sequim, Washington by New Streams Studio
www.newstreamsstudio.com

Unless otherwise noted, scripture quotations have been taken from The Holy Bible, New International Version® NIV®
Copyright © 1973, 1978, 1984 by Biblica, Inc.™

Scripture quotations noted NASB are taken from the New American Standard Bible. Copyright © 1960, 1962, 1963, 1968, 1971, 1972, 1973, 1975, 1977 by the Lockman Foundation.

Scripture quotations have been italicized intentionally throughout this book with the intention of emphasis.

Permission is herein granted to reproduce portions of this book as long as the reproduction is not intended for financial gain. For any further questions, please contact the publisher at the above web address.

TABLE OF CONTENTS

FOREWORD V

PREFACE IX

THE GOSPEL OF THE KINGDOM OF GOD 1

FROM THE IMAGE TO THE LIKENESS OF GOD 27

THE FALL OF MAN 51

THE CROSS 77

SONSHIP 105

SPIRITUAL LIFE 149

SPIRITUAL FRUIT AND SPIRITUAL GIFTS 173

THREE COMPARTMENTS OF MAN
AND THE WORK OF SANCTIFICATION 197

DISCIPLINED INTO HOLINESS 215

THE ORDER OF MELCHIZEDEK 239

MINISTRY OF THE NEW COVENANT 275

THE BODY OF CHRIST
AND OUR ROLES IN IT 295

APPENDIX A 327

TESTIMONIALS 329

FOREWORD

The Seed has had a profound impact on the lives of many here. Personally, it has helped me to recognize the fundamental principles that weave throughout all of the scriptures, but are not elsewhere presented as building blocks which assemble a picture of the true Kingdom Life. New Testament writers borrowed heavily from the Old Testament prophets to help explain the ways of God. These letters which make up the Bible are too often experienced as separate letters with isolated messages. They are too often received as mystery and confusion, along with favorite sound-bite verses to the church system of today.

The Seed helps establish the patterns and purposes of God in a way that brings clarity from the mystery, and reveals the design within God's message that supersedes any particular author's words. God has not changed His mind. He has a plan and is bringing it to fulfillment. *The Seed* gives understanding to the ways in which God has always worked; and, more importantly, the means in which He is bringing about His Kingdom on Earth as it is in Heaven. Understanding what (and how) He is doing His work allows us to orient our lives to better know and worship Him. In doing so, we turn away from the ways of the world, and from meaningless religion, that we may be made ready to participate in His work.

Beyond using *The Seed* for personal growth, it has been a powerful tool of discipleship in the lives of those who are truly seeking the Lord. Only God can make a person grow in Him, but discipleship is the means He most often uses to grow an infant into a fully matured son. The materials presented in *The Seed* provide a path to walk a person through, in order to better know Christ and Him crucified and to step into the realities of things long seen but never experienced by the greatest of prophets. To lay our lives down—that He might fully manifest His life within us, as an honored son dining at the Father's table. And to take up the inheritance and the ministry of a king and priest in God, as a member of the Body of Christ, to bring the fullness of Glory to God the Father as He has always envisioned.

The Seed grabs our attention immediately by challenging the common understanding of The Gospel. Assuming you have been a believer for some time, start by writing down your understanding of The Gospel. Then, study the first chapter. Notice that the Gospel of the Kingdom preached and taught by Jesus and the New Testament leaders is quite different than what is most often presented in the church of today. Does it differ from your own current understanding?

The plan of God for His people in our day is much bigger than what is currently being experienced by most Christians. Once *The Seed* establishes this, it goes back to the beginning to demonstrate God's eternal purpose for Man. As His purpose for Man is understood within the context of rebellion, judgment, and grace—a Savior arises.

Yes, He is one who redeems the fallen who come to Him for an eternity in Heaven. But is that it? Is that all that He has us here for? No! This is only the beginning. As we now know His plan, we are introduced to the greater realities of what He has for us in the here and now. It's not all daisies and rainbows. There is a cross we are to carry and on which we are to die daily. In order to take up His life, our old life must be laid down. Death is painful, but what's on the other side? Life, true life, is extraordinary.

True life is the life of a son of God. In order to realize the purpose of God in our lives, one must be raised up as a son of God. Jesus was that pattern life as the son of God. Not the only one, rather the first of many sons representing Him to all the world. God intends for you and for all His people to experience the spiritual life in the here and now. Yes, there will be fruit of the Spirit living an enlarged life within you—and yes, there will be gifts, but the spiritual life is not merely about these things. It is about the glory of God filling His House (His people). It is about life with Him, and His life being represented to all of Creation.

The Seed shows how God works to sanctify and discipline His people in order to bring about the realities of His life within us. Beyond this, it pulls back the curtain for us to peer into the mysteries of the Order of Melchizedek, and the ministry that must go forth in order to bring about the Lord's purpose for His people and for all of Creation. As we understand how He is assembling His body, we are made readier to see our own role within it. The very purpose for which we were made.

The Seed is not a book of magic that will bestow all of this upon the reader. I would imagine that the average person who stumbled upon this book would find it quite dull.

However, if your heart has been groaning that there must

be something more; or if God has been speaking into your heart that His plan and purposes are greater than what you are hearing about in a pew; I would urge you to take up this material as a means to seek the Lord for what He would show you. Each principle is backed by scripture. You will have to wrestle with God to find out what He would have you know. This book will not make you mature in God. But this process of seeking the Lord within this context of understanding what He wants to do in the world, and in your life, can lead you beyond what you currently believe is possible.

The Lord is building up His Body. His people must be made ready for Him. Let us rise up and answer His call.

Wes Bridel
www.kingdomcalling.com

PREFACE

This series of writings was first written in 2008.

The Lord urged me to revise them and make them available to the disciples of the Lord Jesus Christ who are seeking a deeper life in the Kingdom of God. I do pray these writings will help their journey into the life of the Kingdom of Christ and the glory of God. This series is not meant to be an in-depth study, but I do hope it will help the readers examine and consider some of the fundamental themes of our spiritual life, as shown in the Scriptures.

Our spiritual life as a son of God is always a personal journey. Even so, God the Father never intended it to be an individual endeavor. Rather He designed it to be nurtured via the provision of the Spirit, fostered in His Household as a member of His Family, and established in the Kingdom of Jesus Christ, the Son of God. Through these writings, I hope to offer a sketch of true spiritual life from a "seed" unto its fruition in the field of the Family and Kingdom Culture of God. For those who want to do a more in-depth study on these topics, I have added questions for meditation and review, as well as some relevant scriptures to the end of each chapter.

Please note that when I use the word "Man" capitalized, I am referring to the concept of man as a race of life in God's original intent, rather than in the common sense of man as a human life. There may be some references that share a similar delineation (i.e., the Fall, the Old Covenant, the New

Covenant, Word, Body of Christ, etc.).

My special thanks go to:

- Brother Wes Bridel and Sister Kara Bridel, who helped me with the first draft and edit around the year of 2008
- Brother Tim Pinson Jr. and Brother Dasagen Moodley, who helped me with the second draft before we posted it on the Kingdom Age site (kingdomage.org)
- Brother Ben Lowe, Brother Tim Pinson Jr., Brother John Cochran, Sister Katy Cochran, Sister Cheryl Lowe, and Sister Elaine Cochran for the editing and reviewing of this book
- Sister Elaine Cochran, our wonderful designer, for her artistic and elegant endeavors

All these dear brothers and sisters have helped me tremendously with my English and have enriched our discussions here.

Now may peace and grace from God the Father in heaven and the Lord Jesus Christ be with you now and forever. Amen.

Immanuel Sun
www.kingdomage.org
February 22, 2017
Port Angeles, Washington, USA

1

THE GOSPEL OF THE KINGDOM OF GOD

OVERVIEW

In this chapter, we will give a brief presentation of the Gospel of the Kingdom of God:

- The abnormal phenomenon of the contemporary gospel (The Gospel of Salvation)

- The gospel in the New Testament (The Gospel of the Kingdom of God)

- The essence of The Gospel of the Kingdom

THE GOSPEL OF SALVATION

Today, in many areas of Christianity, the Gospel of the Kingdom of God is coming more and more to the center of attention and emphasis. The consensus is a revelation that the contemporary gospel we have heard and preached around the world for most of the Church Age, even after the Reformation, has fallen short in presenting the fullness of the "Good News." Sin, forgiveness, repentance unto faith in Jesus Christ, heaven and hell, and the gifts and power of the Holy Spirit have been the topics of teaching. These have been regarded as "sound doctrines." Seldom have we heard the gospel preached in the context of the Kingdom of God, and rarely has it been preached as the true reality that comes down from heaven. Instead, what we often hear is a message of salvation—the core of which is still centered around "the interests of man," in understanding and practice. It could be referred to as "half of the gospel," and some have been bold enough to denounce it as a false gospel.

This "half or false gospel" tends to produce, within a man, the idolatry of humanistic love rather than the love of God. As a result, the religious man cherishes values that appeal to the morals and to the "wellbeing" of man—values that are based on a righteousness by human effort, rather than a righteousness rooted in and ministered from the Kingdom of God. Therefore, he upholds a world view of rights and wrongs based on human experiences and human intellect. He appropriates the ideals of life from the traditions and philosophies of man, rather than from divine revelation through a living relationship with a living God, according to His plan and His pleasure. Because of this, man will default himself to seek a form of "godliness" through social or religious duties and outer appearances. He continues on in life with an unchanged, earthly nature. Paul called it the carnal or worldly nature—the life of a lowly, created being rather than as a regenerated spiritual being that is undergoing a transformation from glory to glory. Only when one possesses such a spiritual reality and grows in the true spiritual life, could he then be perfected into the very life of his Creator. This is to be accomplished by the partaking of God's divine nature, which is embodied in the Man of Christ. Let us translate this into biblical language. The former gospel (the Gospel of Salvation) is by and large for the "love of self," "righteousness by the law," "wisdom from below," "the sinful nature of man," or life as a "son of Adam." The latter gospel (the Gospel of the Kingdom) is for the "love of God," "righteousness in the Kingdom of God," "wisdom from above," "the divine nature of God," and life as a "son of God."

GOSPEL OF SALVATION	GOSPEL OF THE KINGDOM
• for the love of self • righteousness by the law • wisdom from below • the sinful nature of man • life as a son of Adam	• for the love of God • righteousness in the Kingdom of God • wisdom from above • the divine nature of God • life as a son of God

In order to further show this contrast, let us give a brief version of the "Gospel of Salvation" according to the former ways, or human tradition:

Man (Adam and Eve) fell when he willfully disobeyed God when tempted by the serpent (Satan). They ate the fruit from the tree of the knowledge of good and evil, thus "sinned" against God and were judged by Him. The consequence of this sin was that they would die and lose access to eternal life. God expelled them from the Garden of Eden and they had to "labor" to make a living. Moreover, everyone who is born of Adam is born in sin and will die and spend eternity in hell. So, God, by His grace, sent His only begotten Son, Jesus Christ, to become a man. He was born of a virgin and died on the cross, thus paying the penalty for our sins and atoning for them. If we believe in Him, confess and repent of our sins, receive Him as our Savior and Lord, and are baptized in the name of the Father, the Son, and the Holy Spirit, then we are saved from sin and death. He will give us eternal life. We will not go to hell, but will be with Him in heaven. Jesus Christ will come back from heaven and raise us up, or "rapture" us when He appears. We then will have eternal life and enjoy His love as a family forever: free from pain, sorrow, and illness. Some even boldly state that our loved ones will be with us in heaven and live with us forever.

To tell you the truth, this almost sounds like folklore compared to the gospel that was preached by Jesus and his disciples.

The life we are given through our faith in Christ Jesus was never intended to be—in God's mind—an extension of our earthly life, even with its best ideals and intentions. Yes, we are saved from hell, but not necessarily reserved for heaven in its present state. Yes, we will be resurrected and have a new body, but it will be a spiritual body, or rather a spiritual being. Yes, Christ will come and free us from pain and sorrow, but more than that, we will also enjoy his glory and his power as we are transformed into his very nature. We will more than belong to God's Family, we will also reign with Him in His Kingdom as kings and priests.

To be "saved" is only the first step of our Christian walk. To grow into maturity, or into the perfect image and likeness of God the Father (which is eternal life in Christ Jesus), is His true intention.

In a sense, the Gospel of Salvation really does only amount to "half of the gospel" at best. There is so much more to the true Life of God!

THE PREACHING OF "THE GOSPEL OF THE KINGDOM OF GOD" IN THE NEW TESTAMENT

If the gospel is not merely about the salvation of human souls, then what is it about? The New Testament states it clearly. It is about the Kingdom of God. Let us look at the gospel preached by some major New Testament characters to gain a clear understanding of this.

John the Baptist

> **MATTHEW 3:1–2**
> *¹ In those days John the Baptist came, preaching in the Desert of Judea ² and saying, "Repent, for the kingdom of heaven is near."*

In the Old Testament prophecies (Malachi 3:1, Isaiah 40:3–5), a forerunner of the Messiah is mentioned and is designated as the messenger who will proclaim the coming of the Messianic Kingdom. In Matthew chapter 3 and John chapters 1 and 3, we can see that John the Baptist intentionally preached a message of repentance. He baptized people so that they would be prepared to receive the King, a king who was coming with His Kingdom. When the baffled rulers and scholars of the day sent messengers to ask John who he was, he plainly denied their imagination to treat him as the Prophet mentioned by Moses.

However, he pointed people to Jesus by declaring that he was both the Lamb of God and the Son of God (or the Messiah). John testified about Jesus and deemed himself unworthy to even be his servant—to untie Jesus' sandals. He encouraged others to follow the Messiah by saying that he took great joy in being a friend of the Groom and giving them over to marry Jesus as his Bride—that is, to become his disciples. He said that his own ministry must decrease, and that Jesus' (his ministry and Kingdom) must increase.

Surely the Kingdom of God, as foreseen and longed for in ages past, had now come, and was to increase and overcome all things that had not been already subdued by it. As the greatest of all prophets, John knew that he was not to compare himself to even the least of those who belong to the Kingdom of the Son of God.

For John, his whole life and ministry was given for this sole purpose: to testify about Jesus, and prepare others to receive the teaching and the Kingdom that come with him. John, although he was a great, godly, and spiritual man, was not granted the privilege during his earthly life to be included as a citizen of the Kingdom of the Son of God, nor a son of the Household of God the Father. This is clearly illustrated by our Lord Jesus and his disciples: the experience of one of the twelve disciples was a privilege granted by the grace of God that had not been granted to those who had gone before them. A privilege to hear, to see, and to enter into the Kingdom of God. John wouldn't dare misrepresent the true intention of God, who had sent His only begotten Son to mankind as a sacrificial lamb to take away their sins, so that they could be restored to Him as His own. John was happy to confess Jesus (an unknown, lowly, and common Israelite) as the Savior and the King, even of his own soul. He had longed for the Day of the Lord, and counted it as the greatest honor to serve him as his messenger.

Jesus Christ

LUKE 4:43

⁴³ "I must preach the good news [the gospel] of the kingdom of God to the other cities also; for I was sent for this purpose."

After being baptized by John, endowed with the power of the Holy Spirit, and tempted by the devil in the wilderness for 40 days, Jesus first preached the gospel at the synagogue of his hometown. While reading from the scroll of the prophet Isaiah, he declared that he fulfilled the scripture that he was reading (Isaiah 61), implying that he was the Messiah—the Anointed One after David. Because of such bold and unconventional preaching, the people, who knew his family and his upbringing, refused to accept his testimony. They actually ended up trying to stone him and push him off of a cliff. What a sad start! He then went to the region of Zebulun and Naphtali to fulfill another portion of scripture recorded in Isaiah 9:1–2.

> **MATTHEW 4:17**
> *17 From that time on Jesus began to preach, "Repent, for the kingdom of heaven is near."*

He would now call his disciples and begin to teach them about the Kingdom of God. This fulfilled:

> **ISAIAH 52:7**
> *7 How beautiful on the mountains are the feet of those who bring good news, who proclaim peace, who bring good tidings, who proclaim salvation, who say to Zion, "Your God reigns!"*

His preaching was accompanied by many miracles, signs, and wonders. Even so, at the time not many believed him. His own mother and brothers refused to do so. Jesus was often distressed and sorrowful because of the blindness of his own people. Due to the nature of his teaching, many had a hard time believing his testimony and embracing his life.

Now we can see that it is evident that Jesus instructed others about his Kingdom. There are a few characteristics that marked his teachings as unconventional, and these characteristics go far beyond the manner in which he delivered them.

First, he preached and taught with authority and power.

Demons were silenced, and men of evil intent were stirred

up. Among these, Jesus' disposition was not as friendly and agreeable as many would like to make him out to be. Today, sadly, many circles of Christianity have degraded the teachings of Jesus into nothing more than a social or moral appeal, within the shell of a religious system. We know Jesus would have none of it. Jesus adamantly criticized the religious teachings and practices of the day to the extent that he openly asserted that it was of the devil, and not of God. He made no compromise with the ways of man or with the traditions of their forefathers, nor with their flesh or their carnal mind. He strictly applied the same standard to those who had chosen to be his disciples, which, in many startling ways, ran in contrast to and in conflict with the kind of discipleship practiced by the Pharisees, Sadducees, and even by John the Baptist. Even those who wanted to be taught by him were constantly upset by him or would be upsetting to him. Jesus made many enemies because of the absolute sanctity of his message and because of his stern criticism of the wickedness of mankind. This was especially true in his relationship with the religious leaders of the day, whom he often aggravated when he called them liars and hypocrites.

Second, he was more than a teacher of the Kingdom, he was a practitioner of it.

With great power of the Holy Spirit, he was able to heal the sick, cast out demons, and perform many miracles. He went far beyond just doing that himself. At the direction of his heavenly Father, Jesus selected 12 men and imparted spiritual authority and power to them. He then sent them out to preach the Kingdom of God. This is recorded in Matthew 10 and Luke 9. After this, Jesus sent out his 72 disciples (as recorded in Luke 10) with the same mission. He wanted them to experience the power of the Holy Spirit for themselves and to be strengthened in their faith in the truths he had taught them about the authority and power of the Kingdom of God. Jesus desired that the teachings and the ministry of eternal life in God would become their conviction and their passion as well.

Here is something worth noticing: Today, many people get confused with the purpose and the work of the power of the Holy Spirit, treating it as an end unto itself, rather than as a means to an end. This is a very sad and misleading way to treat the Holy Spirit. Jesus actually spoke severe warnings against it, which are recorded in Luke 10:17–23.

Third, Jesus constantly had to deal with others' flesh in order to open up their spiritual eyes and ears to receive his teachings.

Such teachings can only be appropriated as spiritual wisdom and understanding. Often, their lack of awareness of the spiritual nature of his teachings made the disciples oblivious to the reality that they were on the forefront of a merciless and forceful war waging between the Kingdom of Light and the Kingdom of Darkness. The devil would seize every opportunity to deter their advancement as the sons of God, and constantly seek to disrupt their course in the seeking of the Kingdom of God. This is often done through the instrumentality of man's flesh, even amongst the disciples. It proved to be a very laborious endeavor on our Lord's part—because the disciples were slow to apprehend their life in such a context, and were reluctant to engage with him in this way of discipleship. With the preaching of the gospel, the advancement of the Kingdom stirred up great conflicts both in heaven and on earth. Yet the disciples, as recorded by their own testimonies in the four gospels, were often clueless about it. Sometimes they were even used by the evil one to obstruct the work of the Lord. Jesus declared openly that his work was to do the will of his Father and to undo the works of the devil. The battlefield of this great conflict in which he labors for a harvest is not only in the heavenly and spiritual realms, but also in the minds and hearts of man. Thus, Jesus was facing resistance not only from outside of his camp, but also from within.

Later, even among his disciples, those whom he called friends and brothers—Judas Iscariot betrayed him; and the others either abandoned him or denied him around the time of his crucifixion. This fulfilled what was prophesied in Psalm 69:19–28 when Jesus prayed for those who persecuted him: "Father, forgive them, for they do not know what they are doing."

Our Lord chose to fulfill the will of his Father and keep the truth of his message to the uttermost, even to the point of death on a cross, as one being accursed by God Himself. This is completely the opposite of what man had assumed the Messiah (the Anointed One) would be. For this reason, the disciples, at that time, had a hard time embracing him. Many shook their heads and turned away.

Jesus taught his disciples about the Kingdom of God. After his resurrection, he also commissioned them to preach the Gospel of the Kingdom and to make disciples in all nations in the same way that he had discipled them. After tarrying in Jerusalem for a while, they were "clothed with power from on high" as he had promised them.

ACTS 1:3

³ After his suffering, he showed himself to these men and gave many convincing proofs that he was alive. He appeared to them over a period of forty days and spoke about the kingdom of God.

LUKE 24:45-49

⁴⁵ Then he opened their minds so they could understand the Scriptures. ⁴⁶ He told them, "This is what is written: The Christ will suffer and rise from the dead on the third day, ⁴⁷ and repentance and forgiveness of sins will be preached in his name to all nations, beginning at Jerusalem. ⁴⁸ You are witnesses of these things. ⁴⁹ I am going to send you what my Father has promised; but stay in the city until you have been clothed with power from on high."

MATTHEW 28:16-20

¹⁶ Then the eleven disciples went to Galilee, to the mountain where Jesus had told them to go. ¹⁷ When they saw him, they worshiped him; but some doubted. ¹⁸ Then Jesus came to them and said, "All authority in heaven and on earth has been given to me. ¹⁹ Therefore go and make disciples of all nations, baptizing them in the name of the Father and of the Son and of the Holy Spirit, ²⁰ and teaching them to obey everything I have commanded you. And surely I am with you always, to the very end of the age."

The Apostles

In book of Acts as well as in the epistles written by the apostles, we can easily recognize that the message that they preached was also the Gospel of the Kingdom of God.

As they waited in Jerusalem, following specific instructions from the Lord, they received the out-pouring of the Holy

Spirit on the day of Pentecost. The Church was thus born and their mission commenced. On that meaningful day, in the face of many false accusations and a great commotion, Peter, endowed with the power of the Holy Spirit, preached the gospel (Acts 2). He preached with such passion, insight, and conviction that his audience felt as if their hearts had been pierced by a sharp sword (see Hebrews 4:12). They were undone. The core of Peter's message is that the Jews had just crucified their Messiah because they were not able to perceive the nature of the Kingdom of God. Three-thousand in Jerusalem were convicted and believed in the name of the Lord Jesus that day.

Peter and other apostles worked many miracles as they continued to preach about their Lord and His Kingdom in the face of great opposition from the religious establishment of the day. They never shrank back. The power of God changed their whole being, so that they became living expressions of the power of a new life, which transformed them from religious piety into sons of the living God. They feared not death nor opposition, as the conviction of the truth of the Kingdom of God and the power of the Holy Spirit enabled them to be "not of this world even though they were in the world."

However, in the early stages, the ministry of the apostles was mostly confined to the Jews. They had yet to embrace and launch into the Lord's mission to evangelize and disciple all peoples of the world. They were still doubtful of God's intention, that even the Gentiles, those "defiled" in the eyes of the Jews, were now equally qualified by their faith in Christ Jesus to receive such a great salvation. To break this mold, God transformed the life of a unique personality in order to bring the Gospel of the Kingdom to the gentile world.

Saul, later known as Paul, was a devout and well-educated Pharisee. He was very zealous in the traditions of his forefathers, so much so that he volunteered to persecute the followers of Jesus. As Paul was traveling to Damascus to carry out his ruthless pursuit, the Lord ambushed him in an encounter that would forever change his life. Through this unexpected experience with the Lord, he became a disciple. The Lord called him to preach the gospel to the Gentiles. From that day on, Paul never turned back. With every fiber of his being, he labored amongst the Gentiles for the Kingdom of God, preaching and teaching the gospel wherever he was sent. In only ten years, he laid the foundation of ten churches in the major cities of the Roman world, especially in the area of Asia Minor.

The faithful servants of God spurred a movement of great magnitude, and they fundamentally shook the Roman world—the most powerful and civilized empire at that time in history. In about 300 years, even Rome endorsed Christianity officially. What an amazing God! And how wonderful His ways!

THE ESSENCE OF THE GOSPEL OF THE KINGDOM OF GOD

In conclusion, let us revisit a brief summary of the Gospel of the Kingdom of God:

In the beginning, God created man in His own image and likeness. His intention was, and is, that His Family would be comprised of many sons, with whom He would share His glory. It was for this reason that He created all the heavens and the earth and everything in them. He gave Adam and Eve the right to rule the creation on His behalf, and He commanded them to multiply after their own kind and to subdue everything. The Lord walked with them and instructed them in His wisdom, in hopes that they would learn His ways and mature into His nature as they fellowshipped together. But man rebelled and was deceived by the serpent, the devil, to seek their own interests and wisdom. They fell into temptation and partook of the fruit from the tree of the knowledge of good and evil— thereby, seeking the likeness of God in a way that He had spoken against. As the result of their sin, they were expelled from God's presence and were not allowed to eat from the tree of life. Thus, sin entered the world through Adam, and with it, death. The two, sin and death, became the ruling powers that the devil used to rule the whole world. Man, being subjected to this Kingdom of Darkness and its depravity, became a lost race, without God and without hope.

At just the right time, God, by His foreknowledge, sent His only begotten Son. Born of a virgin, he became a man of flesh and blood, the last Adam. He tasted our pain and sorrow, the result of sin and death, as a man. More than that, He willingly died as sin (or as a right sacrifice for sin) on our behalf. He took our sin upon Himself and was crucified on a cross, not only at the hand of his own people (the Jews), but also the Gentiles (the Romans). In essence, He took on Himself the wrath that was due to us. Because He did this, He can forgive the sins of those who repent and believe in Him. He is indeed the Son of God who takes away the sin of the world.

After he died, He went to the Deep, and took the keys of Hades and Death. By this, he restored the hope of eternal life to those who put their faith in him, once and for all. Moreover, he also ascended to God's throne in Heaven and sat down at God's right hand as the rightful heir and King of Kings. From this place, he can grant authority and power, given to him by the Father, to those who will become his Church—so that they might subdue everything under him by overcoming the opposition of the evil one and his agents. Whoever believes in him and in his Kingdom, will be given the gift of the Holy Spirit, and thereby eternal life. They will be included as citizens of his Kingdom, and members of the Family of God.

Through Christ's Church, which is the embodiment of his Kingdom as well as the Family of his Father on earth and in heaven, Jesus will subdue everything under his feet. When he has done this, he will hand his Kingdom back to the Father, who will fill Himself all in all.

SCRIPTURES

The Gospel of the Kingdom of God

MATTHEW 4:17
17 From that time on Jesus began to preach, "Repent, for the kingdom of heaven is near."

—In the beginning of Jesus' ministry

MATTHEW 10:7
7 As you [the disciples] go, preach this message: 'The kingdom of heaven is near.'

—During Jesus' ministry

ACTS 28:31
31 He [Paul] proclaimed the kingdom of God and taught about the Lord Jesus Christ—with all boldness and without hindrance!

—The early church

MATTHEW 24:14
14 And this gospel of the kingdom will be preached in the whole world as a testimony to all nations, and then the end will come.

—The end times

The Essence of the Gospel

EPHESIANS 1:3–14
3 Praise be to the God and Father of our Lord Jesus Christ, who has blessed us in the heavenly realms with every spiritual blessing in Christ. 4 For he chose us in him before the creation of the world to be holy and blameless in

his sight. In love ⁵ *he predestined us to be adopted as his sons through Jesus Christ, in accordance with his pleasure and will—*
⁶ *to the praise of his glorious grace, which he has freely given us in the One he loves.* ⁷ *In him we have redemption through his blood, the forgiveness of sins, in accordance with the riches of God's grace* ⁸ *that he lavished on us with all wisdom and understanding.* ⁹ *And he made known to us the mystery of his will per his good pleasure, which he purposed in Christ,*
¹⁰ *to be put into effect when the times will have reached their fulfillment—to bring all things in heaven and on earth together under one head, even Christ.*
¹¹ *In him we were also chosen, having been predestined according to the plan of him who works out everything in conformity with the purpose of his will,* ¹² *in order that we, who were the first to hope in Christ, might be for the praise of his glory.* ¹³ *And you also were included in Christ when you heard the word of truth, the gospel of your salvation. Having believed, you were marked in him with a seal, the promised Holy Spirit,*
¹⁴ *who is a deposit guaranteeing our inheritance until the redemption of those who are God's possession—to the praise of his glory.*

1 CORINTHIANS 15:20-28

²⁰ *But Christ has indeed been raised from the dead, the firstfruits of those who have fallen asleep.* ²¹ *For since death came through a man, the resurrection of the dead comes also through a man.* ²² *For as in Adam all die, so in Christ all will be made alive.* ²³ *But each in his own turn: Christ, the firstfruits; then, when he comes, those who belong to him.*
²⁴ *Then the end will come, when he hands over the kingdom to God the Father after he has destroyed all dominion, authority and power.* ²⁵ *For he must reign until he has put all his enemies under his feet.* ²⁶ *The last enemy to be destroyed is death.* ²⁷ *For he "has put everything under his feet." Now when it says that "everything" has been put under him, it is clear that this does not include God himself, who put everything under Christ.* ²⁸ *When he has done this, then the Son himself will be made subject to him who put everything under him, so that God may be all in all.*

QUESTIONS FOR REVIEW

1. What stands out to you when you read this chapter?

___

2. What kind of gospel have you heard before? Have you ever heard anyone concentrate on the Kingdom of God in his or her presenting of the gospel to you?

___

3. What gospel did Jesus Christ and his disciples preach? Can you give a brief description of it?

___

QUESTIONS
FOR MEDITATION & APPLICATION

1. Every religious or philosophical world view confronts the same basic questions. How do you now answer these "tough" questions in light of the Gospel of the Kingdom of God?

- Where are you from? (What is the source of your life?)

_____

_____

- Who are you?

_____

_____

- Why are you here?

_____

_____

- Where are you going?

_____

_____

Now read this verse:

GENESIS 1:28

²⁸ God blessed them and said to them, "Be fruitful and increase in number; fill the earth and subdue it. Rule over the fish of the sea and the birds of the air and over every living creature that moves on the ground."

2. Can you give a brief explanation of what God means when He is talking about subduing and ruling?

_____

_____

_____

3. Continue to ponder the above verse. Now, do you think that man, in general, currently has the position and power to do what God commanded in this present age?

_____

_____

_____

4. Now that you have briefly considered the concept of the Kingdom of God, please contemplate on how it will impact your life in these areas:

- Your spiritual life

_____

_____

- Your life in the world

_____

_____

- Your life in the Body of Christ

_____

_____

2

FROM THE IMAGE TO THE LIKENESS OF GOD

OVERVIEW

In this section, we will discuss how God created man, and what He intended for man when He created him:

- Why God created man

- Created in the image of God

- From the image of God to the likeness of God

WHY GOD CREATED MAN

MATTHEW 20:16
16 "So the last will be first, and the first will be last."

Most of us are familiar with this teaching of Jesus. He was admonishing his disciples not to strive for position and honor, rather that they should learn to serve and love one another. Yet this lesson is also one of the keys to unlocking the mysteries of the Kingdom of God. It explains why He taught them this Kingdom principle.

Aside from its obvious prophetic implications, it also points us to the omnipresence of God. Time (or the history of creation) does not have any bearing on Him, but serves as the means to His end, which is to bring about His Kingdom and the fulfillment of His plan concerning His Son. God knows the end from the beginning and has set everything in motion in His foreknowledge.

REVELATION 1:8
8 "I am the Alpha and the Omega," says the Lord God, "who is, and who was, and who is to come, the Almighty."

The business of God the Father, a work entrusted to the Son, and administered by the Holy Spirit, is to glorify His Son, thus glorifying Himself. God will also glorify those who, like His Son, are perfected into His holiness or eternal life. This is accomplished through the perfection of manhood by the Spirit of sonship and into its fullness (maturity), which is none other than the Father's eternal life. It is patterned after and revealed by Jesus Christ who became a man on our behalf. The Son bears the Father's perfect image and likeness, he is the "exact representation of the Father" (Hebrews 1:3). In essence, through our faith in the Son, the Father will adopt us as sons into His Family, bestowing on us more than just His blood-line (life), but also His very name (glory) when we have matured into His divine nature or godliness. For this very reason, Jesus Christ came and died, so that he can take away our sins and free us into this abundant life.

Jesus Christ is also acting on our behalf as our advocate and mediator against Satan, who is ever opposing and challenging the standing of Jesus Christ and those who belong to him. When he was raised from the dead and ascended into heaven, he sat down at the right hand of the Father, and the Father gave him all authority and power. He was given not only the power to overcome Satan, but also the power to subdue all things under his feet. Jesus will do this for the Church and through the Church, which is his Body, with him being the Head of this spiritual Man. Therefore, this is the work of the Father and the Son: to multiply or increase their divine life through the perfection of man, in the Spirit—thus establishing the Kingdom of God on earth as it is in Heaven. This is for the glory and the pleasure of the Father. In other words, this is what will glorify God and please Him.

God always intended for His Word to become flesh. Jesus Christ was the perfect seed, the firstborn of the Spirit of sonship in the form of a mortal man, who by the power of resurrection became the firstfruits among many who are also called and destined to conform into this life of sonship (1 Corinthians 15:23). In this light, it is quite illuminating to carefully consider the way God created man in the first place.

It should be noted that across the ages, God never intended to leave man outside of His counsel and wisdom. Man has always been the crown of His creation, the delight of His heart, and the object of His affection. God's will is that man would be able to put aside all that has veiled his sight and marred his understanding, and come back to Him to be taught by Him like a son would be taught by his own father. This is God's goodwill to man when He created him, and is the end (the mark, or the target) of His work towards man. God reserved the full measure of His nature, power, and wisdom as the inheritance for man when he is perfected in Him. It is then inevitable that a disciple of Jesus Christ, after receiving new life by the Holy Spirit, is to be taught and disciplined (or discipled by God Himself) to grow in His counsel, wisdom and favor, and to partake of His divine nature and power—embodied in the life of His Son. In the end, he will be changed into God's own glory or His very being, becoming one with Him and in Him through His Son.

This is the journey from His image to His likeness, the journey of sonship.

Indeed, God's primary purpose of creation is to have sons. They would be proved in justice and righteousness, worthy of His name, and endowed with glory and honor. In this they are to share His Kingdom as co-heirs with Christ Jesus and reign with him as kings and priests over all that He created and will create. Beyond this, they will share His nature and desire and become the perfect recipients and givers of His love and His wisdom, being able to offer this "new life" to those who are to learn of Him (become the disciples of Jesus Christ). All creation will be judged by the sons of God, and will learn of their Creator from them.

Here is a quote from a friend, Mark Reece, who wrote in the article, *In His Image*:

> "One of the most startling of the mysteries which has been revealed to the Church through Jesus Christ is that from the very beginning, God purposed to have many sons. It was revealed in fact that the Lamb was slain from before the foundation of the world (Revelation 13). Not only was He slain from the foundation of the world and revealed in the fullness of time, but the book of Hebrews tells us that it was for the purpose of bringing many sons to glory (Hebrews 2). This, then, is the purpose of God which underlies and undergirds all of the subsequent facts surrounding the creation of man. Knowing that God's primary purpose in creation was to have many sons changes how we think about man's being, and must also impact the understanding we have of mankind being created in the image and likeness of God."[a]

To know this End, we must turn back to the Beginning.

---

[a] Reece, Mark. "In His Image."

CREATED IN HIS IMAGE

Now let's turn to Genesis, the book of beginnings, to look at how God created man after the first five days of creation:

GENESIS 1:26–27
26 Then God said, "Let us make man in our image, in our likeness, and let them rule over the fish of the sea and the birds of the air, over the livestock, over all the earth, and over all the creatures that move along the ground." 27 So God created man in his own image, in the image of God he created him; male and female he created them.

GENESIS 2:7
7 Then the Lord God formed the man from the dust of the ground and breathed into his nostrils the breath of life, and the man became a living being.

GENESIS 2:20-24
20 So the man gave names to all the livestock, the birds of the air and all the beasts of the field. But for Adam no suitable helper was found. 21 So the Lord God caused the man to fall into a deep sleep; and while he was sleeping, he took one of the man's ribs and closed up the place with flesh. 22 Then the Lord God made a woman from the rib he had taken out of the man, and he brought her to the man. 23 The man said,
"This is now bone of my bones and flesh of my flesh; she shall be called 'woman,' for she was taken out of man."
24 For this reason a man will leave his father and mother and be united to his wife, and they will become one flesh.

Notice that when God created man, He intended that man will

be made in their image and their likeness. (Here usually it is to be understood the plural name of God implies all persons in the Godhead: Father, Son, and the Spirit.) And man was given the role and responsibility to rule over all that was created for him.

Also, please notice in verse 27:

> 1. Only man, both male and female, were created in "his own image."

> 2. How interesting that the plural denotation of God is changed to be singular. In this singular personality, two genders or two characteristics of man, were created in mankind.

> 3. Here also observe that only "image" is mentioned, but not "likeness."

I will not cover every school of thought concerning these few verses (see Appendix A). They are simple yet profound, plain yet intriguing. For now, we will only give a few key observations of God's eternal plan for mankind and His Kingdom. My hope is that this will help to unlock your understanding of the nature and the work of the Kingdom of God.

- God created man to be His son, and He intended to endow the soul of man with the Spirit of sonship. With it, he becomes a spiritual being, and is enabled to hear the counsel of the Father, who is the invisible God, and see the reality (truth) of the Kingdom of His Son, which is from heaven and of a spiritual nature and substance.

He is destined to be taught by the Father as His son. Through this fellowship with the Father, a son is able to mature into the nature of God.

- It was God's glory and good pleasure to create man out of earthly elements (dust) and form him into an organic being (flesh and blood) with a higher life (a living soul) than other creations. In a sense, there is nothing special about man in his physical makeup. Yet, by God's breath (the life of His Spirit), man was given a soul that was capable of appreciating and receiving love and wisdom, made to be a perfect vessel for the workmanship of the Godhead. This work is to be accomplished in his heart, his soul, his mind, and even in his earthly body. Man is destined to become the temple (tent, house, tabernacle, or dwelling place) of the Holy Spirit, and the glory of God. Man and God will become one through the perfection of manhood via the Spirit of sonship, both individually and collectively.

- God intended for man to rule his creation and to administer His justice and righteousness, wisdom and love, and thus become the image and likeness of Himself to all creation. All of creation is to learn of God and yield to God's love and sovereignty through man's perfect obedience, having become the exact representation of His Father as His son. In other words, man was created to be priests and kings on God's behalf: to mediate and to teach all creation the knowledge of God and make them have peace with Him, come into His presence and be changed into His glory as well. Indeed, it is ever the Father's desire that heaven and earth be filled with the knowledge and the glory of Himself.

DESTINED FOR HIS LIKENESS

Now we can see that when God created man, man was only created in "His image," but not yet in His likeness (Genesis 1:27). Such a distinction is often obscured by many commentators. I think the reason is because they have not fully grasped the full extent of God's mystery in creating man. In other words, they are still unsettled with some of the basics of the mind of God: what man is, and what God's plan is for him. For some of our dear readers, this may seem to be a bold statement, if not an arrogant one. Hopefully it will prove otherwise as we turn back to contemplate the teachings of Jesus, which were also passed on to the early church by the apostles. Today, many scholars try hard to categorize New Testament teachings with authorship, as if man's personal traits would define God's eternal truth and wisdom. Let's brush aside such cloudy thinking, and consider the true source of such a wisdom and acknowledge that this kind of approach is "from below," or earthly. It depends on human intellect and speculation, and is not the kind of wisdom that Jesus and the early apostles enjoyed. They, on the contrary, were all taught by a wisdom that comes "from above." They never tried to teach their own doctrines or revelations. What was revealed to, and taught by them, was plain and clear. One of the keys to unlock the secrets or the mysteries of the Kingdom of God, is that God created man in His own image, and He intended to give him the Spirit of sonship, so that he could fellowship with Him and thereby become "like" Him. This truth, that Jesus is the Son of God, is the rock or foundation of our faith in God (see Matthew 16:13–20). In doing so, man will be transformed into the likeness of God, thus becoming one with the Father and with the Son. This was plainly shared by Jesus, Peter, John and Paul in diverse portions of the scriptures.

Here are a few key observations:

> 1. When God created man, He gave him the full faculty to be able to fellowship with Him. This implies that man can see, hear, and understand God. He enjoys the full spiritual capacity and ability to commune with God, just as he enjoys the physical, mental and moral capacity to sense and analyze the natural world. He can memorize and reflect what happens in time. He can form, process, express, and retract thoughts, emotions, feelings—even organize them into patterns of thinking, and thus rationalize his judgments, attitudes, behaviors, and decisions if he so chooses. He can judge and discern within behavioral, moral, relational, communal, and social standards. This enables him to enjoy the confidence to decide what is moral, right, just, reasonable, etc. offering unto him a sense of knowing what is right and wrong. He can even develop these further to embody, practice, and regulate them as conventions or principles (stated or not) as in communal settings. This ability is by itself a great gift from God, and truly is a blessing. It is God's desire to help him achieve just this, as testified by the spirit and heart of the Law of Moses, and by Jesus' teachings. God wants man to live out and to fully embody His love, righteousness, and wisdom.
>
> However, when man's mind is skewed away from, (and remains ignorant of) His divine nature and wisdom, this gift then will be abused or misused to produce, endorse, justify, and develop his own righteousness. He will then have to acquire and develop wisdom on his own and rely

on strengths or powers that are not from God, be it of his own or from the evil one. He then excludes himself from the counsel and wisdom of God, and won't be able to live in and by God's divine power, even the power of His eternal life. In the Father's sight, he is a son that has lost his way. He is deceived and held captive by the evil one through his own evil desires in a corrupt world, as Peter would put it. His life is sin (missing the mark) and his end is death (decay, corruption).

2. Now, the natural or physical aspect of man's capability to learn and strive for understanding and intelligence is only the tip of the iceberg, and simply a shadow of what God endowed man with in terms of the spiritual. Just a side note here: Brother Watchmen Nee has a book entitled, *The Latent Power of the Soul*. In it, he mentions that the soul or mind of man would be able to avail psychic power for his selfish and vile purposes.[b] Spiritualism and witchcraft are of such a nature. But these are proved to be an illegal, if not destructive, pathway to avail spiritual power and understanding. Such wisdom, by its nature and source, is base and very limited when compared with the rich, pure, and glorious wisdom of God, which is embodied in and ministered in His Household and the Kingdom of His Son. He will freely give it to us if we repent from our wicked ways, receive the Lordship of Jesus Christ, and hold on to the faith preached in the gospel until the end.

---

[b] Nee, Watchman. *The Latent Power of The Soul.* Christian Fellowship Publishers, 1972.

3. God created man to be able to fellowship with Him as a son would with his father, and attain His eternal life. It was the tree of the knowledge of good and evil that Adam and Eve were forbidden to eat, not the tree of life. When Jesus died on the cross, he took the blame or the curse (cursed is a man who dies on a tree), and was lifted up as a symbol of shame, thus satisfying the just God for the price of death in regard to sin. In this, he becomes our redemption, forgiveness, atonement, justification, righteousness and even sanctification and glorification. If we hold on to our faith, we will be fully restored back to the Father, and the privilege of His fellowship and love. He indeed is the Way. However, it takes a process for this pattern of life to be actualized in our own spiritual life in time and space. In the teachings of Jesus and his apostles, this process is described as our spiritual journey of sanctification, glorification, maturity, transformation, the renewal of our minds, cleansing of our old self, etc. The essence is all the same. That is, to partake in the nature of God and to be changed from a natural man into a mature spiritual son. We are to grow from His image into His likeness.

In this light, we can see just how much man had lost from the Fall—almost everything that mattered according to the goodwill of God and the wellbeing of himself!

SCRIPTURES

Why God Created Man

EPHESIANS 1:3-6

³ Praise be to the God and Father of our Lord Jesus Christ, who has blessed us in the heavenly realms with every spiritual blessing in Christ. ⁴ For he chose us in him before the creation of the world to be holy and blameless in his sight. In love ⁵ he predestined us to be adopted as his sons through Jesus Christ, in accordance with his pleasure and will— ⁶ to the praise of his glorious grace, which he has freely given us in the One he loves.

2 CORINTHIANS 4:18; 5:1-5

¹⁸ So we fix our eyes not on what is seen, but on what is unseen. For what is seen is temporary, but what is unseen is eternal.

¹ Now we know that if the earthly tent we live in is destroyed, we have a building from God, an eternal house in heaven, not built by human hands. ² Meanwhile we groan, longing to be clothed with our heavenly dwelling, ³ because when we are clothed, we will not be found naked. ⁴ For while we are in this tent, we groan and are burdened, because we do not wish to be unclothed but to be clothed with our heavenly dwelling, so that what is mortal may be swallowed up by life. ⁵ Now it is God who has made us for this very purpose and has given us the Spirit as a deposit, guaranteeing what is to come.

HEBREWS 2:10-13

¹⁰ In bringing many sons to glory, it was fitting that God, for whom and through whom everything exists, should make the author of their salvation perfect through suffering. ¹¹ Both the one who makes men holy

and those who are made holy are of the same family. So Jesus is not ashamed to call them brothers. ¹² He says,
"I will declare your name to my brothers; in the presence of the congregation I will sing your praises."
¹³ And again,
"I will put my trust in him."
And again he says,
"Here am I, and the children God has given me."

Created in His Image, Destined for His Likeness

JOHN 10:30-38

³⁰ I and the Father are one."
³¹ Again his Jewish opponents picked up stones to stone him, ³² but Jesus said to them, "I have shown you many good works from the Father. For which of these do you stone me?"
³³ "We are not stoning you for any good work," they replied, "but for blasphemy, because you, a mere man, claim to be God."
³⁴ Jesus answered them, "Is it not written in your Law, 'I have said you are "gods"'? ³⁵ If he called them 'gods,' to whom the word of God came—and Scripture cannot be set aside— ³⁶ what about the one whom the Father set apart as his very own and sent into the world? Why then do you accuse me of blasphemy because I said, 'I am God's Son'? ³⁷ Do not believe me unless I do the works of my Father. ³⁸ But if I do them, even though you do not believe me, believe the works, that you may know and understand that the Father is in me, and I in the Father."

JOHN 14:6-17

⁶ Jesus answered, "I am the way and the truth and the life. No one comes to the Father except through me. ⁷ If you really knew me, you would know my Father as well. From now on, you do know him and

have seen him."
⁸ Philip said, "Lord, show us the Father and that will be enough for us."
⁹ Jesus answered: "Don't you know me, Philip, even after I have been among you such a long time? Anyone who has seen me has seen the Father. How can you say, 'Show us the Father'? ¹⁰ Don't you believe that I am in the Father, and that the Father is in me? The words I say to you are not just my own. Rather, it is the Father, living in me, who is doing his work. ¹¹ Believe me when I say that I am in the Father and the Father is in me; or at least believe on the evidence of the miracles themselves. ¹² I tell you the truth, anyone who has faith in me will do what I have been doing. He will do even greater things than these, because I am going to the Father. ¹³ And I will do whatever you ask in my name, so that the Son may bring glory to the Father. ¹⁴ You may ask me for anything in my name, and I will do it.

¹⁵ "If you love me, you will obey what I command. ¹⁶ And I will ask the Father, and he will give you another Counselor to be with you forever— ¹⁷ the Spirit of truth. The world cannot accept him, because it neither sees him nor knows him. But you know him, for he lives with you and will be in you.

HEBREWS 1:1–13

¹ In the past God spoke to our forefathers through the prophets at many times and in various ways, ² but in these last days he has spoken to us by his Son, whom he appointed heir of all things, and through whom he made the universe. ³ The Son is the radiance of God's glory and the exact representation of his being, sustaining all things by his powerful word. After he had provided purification for sins, he sat down at the right hand of the Majesty in heaven. ⁴ So he became as much superior to the angels as the name he has inherited is superior to theirs.

⁵ For to which of the angels did God ever say,

"You are my Son; today I have become your Father"?
Or again, "I will be his Father, and he will be my Son"?
⁶ And again, when God brings his firstborn into the world, he says,
"Let all God's angels worship him."
⁷ In speaking of the angels he says,
"He makes his angels winds, his servants flames of fire."
⁸ But about the Son he says, "Your throne, O God, will last for ever and ever, and righteousness will be the scepter of your kingdom.
⁹ You have loved righteousness and hated wickedness; therefore God, your God, has set you above your companions by anointing you with the oil of joy."
¹⁰ He also says,
"In the beginning, O Lord, you laid the foundations of the earth, and the heavens are the work of your hands.
¹¹ They will perish, but you remain; they will all wear out like a garment. ¹² You will roll them up like a robe; like a garment they will be changed. But you remain the same, and your years will never end."
¹³ To which of the angels did God ever say,
"Sit at my right hand until I make your enemies a footstool for your feet"?

COLOSSIANS 1:12-20

¹² giving thanks to the Father, who has qualified you to share in the inheritance of the saints in the kingdom of light. ¹³ For he has rescued us from the dominion of darkness and brought us into the kingdom of the Son he loves, ¹⁴ in whom we have redemption, the forgiveness of sins.

¹⁵ He is the image of the invisible God, the firstborn over all creation. ¹⁶ For by him all things were created: things in heaven and on earth, visible and invisible, whether thrones or powers or rulers or authorities; all things were created by him and for him. ¹⁷ He is before all things, and in him all things hold together. ¹⁸ And he is the head of the body,

the church; he is the beginning and the firstborn from among the dead, so that in everything he might have the supremacy. ¹⁹ *For God was pleased to have all his fullness dwell in him,* ²⁰ *and through him to reconcile to himself all things, whether things on earth or things in heaven, by making peace through his blood, shed on the cross.*

2 CORINTHIANS 3:17-18; 4:1-6

¹⁷ *Now the Lord is the Spirit, and where the Spirit of the Lord is, there is freedom.* ¹⁸ *And we, who with unveiled faces all reflect the Lord's glory, are being transformed into his likeness with ever-increasing glory, which comes from the Lord, who is the Spirit.*

¹ *Therefore, since through God's mercy we have this ministry, we do not lose heart.* ² *Rather, we have renounced secret and shameful ways; we do not use deception, nor do we distort the word of God. On the contrary, by setting forth the truth plainly we commend ourselves to every man's conscience in the sight of God.* ³ *And even if our gospel is veiled, it is veiled to those who are perishing.* ⁴ *The god of this age has blinded the minds of unbelievers, so that they cannot see the light of the gospel of the glory of Christ, who is the image of God.* ⁵ *For we do not preach ourselves, but Jesus Christ as Lord, and ourselves as your servants for Jesus' sake.* ⁶ *For God, who said, "Let light shine out of darkness," made his light shine in our hearts to give us the light of the knowledge of the glory of God in the face of Christ.*

2 PETER 1:3-11

³ *His divine power has given us everything we need for life and godliness through our knowledge of him who called us by his own glory and goodness.* ⁴ *Through these he has given us his very great and precious promises, so that through them you may participate in the divine nature and escape the corruption in the world caused by evil desires.* ⁵ *For this very reason, make every effort to add to your faith goodness;*

and to goodness, knowledge; ⁶ and to knowledge, self-control; and to self-control, perseverance; and to perseverance, godliness; ⁷ and to godliness, brotherly kindness; and to brotherly kindness, love. ⁸ For if you possess these qualities in increasing measure, they will keep you from being ineffective and unproductive in your knowledge of our Lord Jesus Christ. ⁹ But if anyone does not have them, he is nearsighted and blind, and has forgotten that he has been cleansed from his past sins.

¹⁰ Therefore, my brothers, be all the more eager to make your calling and election sure. For if you do these things, you will never fall, ¹¹ and you will receive a rich welcome into the eternal kingdom of our Lord and Savior Jesus Christ.

QUESTIONS
FOR REVIEW

1. What stands out to you when you read this chapter?

___

2. What are your thoughts about the true purpose of God in creating man?

___

3. What do you think about the difference between the image of God and the likeness of God?

___

QUESTIONS
FOR MEDITATION & APPLICATION

1. Why did God create you?

2. What does it mean to you that you are created in God's own image?

3. How do you develop your spiritual life into the likeness of God?

4. What does it mean to you to be a "son of God"?

_____

_____

_____

3

THE FALL OF MAN

OVERVIEW

In this chapter, we will discuss the Fall of man and the consequences thereof:

- The Fall of Adam and Eve
- Consequences of the Fall

THE FALL OF ADAM AND EVE

Let us again turn to the book of Genesis to investigate the beginning of all the tragedies of mankind.

In today's world, most people are familiar with this story compared to other times in human history. There are also now more interpretations, whether truthful and helpful or not, that seek to use it to support one's own understanding. Sadly, many are doing so without ever believing in its truthfulness. It seems that few have ever really examined it with a humble heart and appreciated it in the spiritual dimension where it belongs. However, to a large degree, the interpretation of this story reflects one's relationship with God. Without faith in God and a living relationship with Him, spiritual understanding and wisdom can never be attained.

We can also venture to say that, one (even a believer) will not be able to go further in his pursuit of truth and life in the Kingdom of God until the depths of this story, with its implications and applications in our lives, are understood in a very personal way. To move on in spiritual wisdom, we must reconcile our scattered understandings and embrace the spiritual reality. This story of God and man proceeds from such a reality. Its spiritual rules also constitute many of the aspects of the fundamental order and ways in such a reality. It calls for our serious consideration and careful scrutiny. Surely this must be done with a rightful fear or reverence of God and a good faith in His word and His ways.

Similar Stories but Different Results

In this chapter, we will only give this story some key observations while comparing it to the one when Jesus was tested in the wilderness.

> **GENESIS 2:8-9**
> *⁸ Now the Lord God had planted a garden in the east, in Eden; and there he put the man he had formed. ⁹ And the Lord God made all kinds of trees grow out of the ground—trees that were pleasing to the eye and good for food. In the middle of the garden were the tree of life and the tree of the knowledge of good and evil.*

Notice that the trees God gave to man to eat from are not bad. They were pleasing to the eye and good as food.

> **GENESIS 2:15-18**
> *¹⁵ The Lord God took the man and put him in the Garden of Eden to work it and take care of it. ¹⁶ And the Lord God commanded the man, "You are free to eat from any tree in the garden; ¹⁷ but you must not eat from the tree of the knowledge of good and evil, for when you eat of it you will surely die." ¹⁸ The Lord God said, "It is not good for the man to be alone. I will make a helper suitable for him."*

While God withheld nothing good from man, He did withhold what was bad from him. Now, some may wonder why He put a tree there that would cause all the problems and heartache between Him and mankind in the first place. Was it so that man would fall into temptation? Is God also the author of sin and evil? Let's be clear, this kind of questions reveals a fundamental misunderstanding of the nature and the ways of God.

God always desired man to have a trusting and obedient heart towards Him. God's way into eternal life and true fellowship with Him is that man would hear and obey. Some claim God's love is unconditional. This might cause confusion unless we offer a proper definition of what "unconditional" means. For God does have a condition for man to be blessed by Him and to love Him. Jesus taught that man should follow His command out of his love and obedience unto God, which is the essence of "faith in God." The author of Hebrews states that, without such a faith, it is impossible to please God. He unconditionally offers all love, provision, benefit and goodness to mankind, but we have to repent from our wicked ways in order to receive the forgiveness of our sins and the eternal life in Him. God did bless and is blessing every man with the gift of freewill, meaning that man can choose to obey or to rebel against His ways. Note, without such a choice out of freewill there would have been no true obedience. However, in granting man this freewill, God also blesses him with the ability, the grace, and the way to learn to know what to obey and how to obey. This is why He eagerly desires man to fellowship with Him and to be taught by Him. However, this has to be done willingly and not out of compulsion or without any understanding. Do we not know that faith and obedience, by nature, are to be tried and tested?

So is true love. If it is not by choice, especially in the context of sacrificing one's own interest or wellbeing for another, such love is then shallow or even false and cannot be considered as genuine, sincere, or faithful. Man was, from the very beginning, created to be participants and agents of the divine, faithful and pure love of God. Created to be recipients and dispensers of His kind of love both to Himself, to his fellow man, and to all creation. Without this innate ability, there would be no concept of love nor the possibility to practice it. In a way, it would be fair to say that we could not be called "human" when deprived of this ability of love.

In this light, it becomes imperative for us to know that when God created man, He created us with the intention that we are to be perfected into the power and wisdom of His life, which is the pathway for us to be perfected in His love. In essence, God's will and good pleasure is that when we are facing the choice of our own freewill versus His will, we would, out of our love for Him as our caring Father and our trust in Him as the God of all faithfulness and power, choose to obey Him in order to please Him, rather than to satisfy our own desires and pleasures or something other than Him.

We can easily see that the heart of obedience toward his heavenly Father and his God is vividly exemplified by Jesus' interaction with the devil in the wilderness, recorded in Luke 4. Concerning this, the author of Hebrews explains:

> **HEBREWS 2:14-18**
> *[14] Since the children have flesh and blood, he too shared in their humanity so that by his death he might destroy him who holds the power of death—that is, the devil—[15] and free those who all their lives were held in slavery by their fear of death. [16] For surely it is not angels he helps, but Abraham's descendants. [17] For this reason he had to be made like his brothers in every way, in order that he might become a merciful and faithful high priest in service to God, and that he might make atonement for the sins of the people. [18] Because he himself suffered when he was tempted, he is able to help those who are being tempted.*

Adam and Eve failed this test (temptation), as recorded in Genesis 3. Thus, sin and death entered the world, the seed of sonship was snatched away from mankind, and with it—the promise and covenant of eternal life (Matthew 13:18). Even so, Jesus was victorious over the devil and death. Out of obedience, he willingly walked flawlessly—without missing anything—in the will of his heavenly Father. He thus became the perfect sacrifice of atonement for the sins (missing the mark) of all mankind, even of the whole world (cosmos, this creation, or this age). He completely yielded to the will of his Heavenly Father in order to please Him, even to the point of death on the cross.

Now let's read these two stories together:

GENESIS 3:1–13

¹ Now the serpent was more crafty than any of the wild animals the Lord God had made. He said to the woman, "Did God really say, 'You must not eat from any tree in the garden'?"
² The woman said to the serpent, "We may eat fruit from the trees in the garden, ³ but God did say, 'You must not eat fruit from the tree that is in the middle of the garden, and you must not touch it, or you will die.'"
⁴ "You will not surely die," the serpent said to the woman. ⁵ "For God knows that when you eat of it your eyes will be opened, and you will be like God, knowing good and evil."
⁶ When the woman saw that the fruit of the tree was good for food and pleasing to the eye, and also desirable for gaining wisdom, she took some and ate it. She also gave some to her husband, who was with her, and he ate it. ⁷ Then the eyes of both of them were opened, and they realized they were naked; so they sewed fig leaves together and made coverings for themselves.

The Seed

⁸ Then the man and his wife heard the sound of the Lord God as he was walking in the garden in the cool of the day, and they hid from the Lord God among the trees of the garden. ⁹ But the Lord God called to the man, "Where are you?"
¹⁰ He answered, "I heard you in the garden, and I was afraid because I was naked; so I hid."
¹¹ And he said, "Who told you that you were naked? Have you eaten from the tree that I commanded you not to eat from?"
¹² The man said, "The woman you put here with me—she gave me some fruit from the tree, and I ate it."
¹³ Then the Lord God said to the woman, "What is this you have done?" The woman said, "The serpent deceived me, and I ate."

LUKE 4:1–13

¹ Jesus, full of the Holy Spirit, returned from the Jordan and was led by the Spirit in the desert, ² where for forty days he was tempted by the devil. He ate nothing during those days, and at the end of them he was hungry.
³ The devil said to him, "If you are the Son of God, tell this stone to become bread."
⁴ Jesus answered, "It is written: 'Man does not live on bread alone.'"
⁵ The devil led him up to a high place and showed him in an instant all the kingdoms of the world. ⁶ And he said to him, "I will give you all their authority and splendor, for it has been given to me, and I can give it to anyone I want to. ⁷ So if you worship me, it will all be yours."
⁸ Jesus answered, "It is written: 'Worship the Lord your God and serve him only.'"
⁹ The devil led him to Jerusalem and had him stand on the highest point of the temple. "If you are the Son of God," he said, "throw yourself down from here. ¹⁰ For it is written:

> *"'He will command his angels concerning you to guard you carefully;* ¹¹ *they will lift you up in their hands, so that you will not strike your foot against a stone.'"*
> ¹² *Jesus answered, "It says: 'Do not put the Lord your God to the test.'"*
> ¹³ *When the devil had finished all this tempting, he left him until an opportune time.*

What Caused the Fall of Man?

The scriptures tell us that the serpent was crafty, and that the devil used his craftiness to deceive man. Interestingly, God had given man dominion over the serpent before this happened. Adam and Eve should have been able to discern the lies of the serpent, rebuke it, and watch it flee in terror; for man was given the power to not only discern his evil schemes but even to judge him. That is what it means to subdue things under one's authority. The authority and power God gave to man would enable him to judge not only the serpent, but all created things. If we relate this to what Jesus taught in the New Testament, we would know that Adam and Eve were to learn to judge even the angels. In this light, we, as sons of God, should have no fear of the devil, his demons, or evil angels. However, we do need to have the fear of God within us so that we will not disobey God, and allow the devil to gain a foothold in our lives.

Now, let's look closer at the lies the serpent spoke to Eve and compare them with the ones he offered to Jesus:

First, he twisted God's command and tried to lure Eve to deny the goodness of God concerning His provision for them.

Ha! It is about food! Now we know Adam and Eve were enjoying the abundance of the Garden of Eden. In contrast, Jesus had not been able to eat or drink for 40 days. The devil did not even bother to challenge Adam and Eve about whether they were sons of God or not. However, with his perverted reasoning, he shamelessly tried to undermine Jesus' knowledge and confidence as to whether he was truly God's Son. In essence, Satan tried to lure Jesus to forfeit his identity as the Son of God, and thus his birthright and inheritance from God the Father. If we take a closer look at the story, the devil even tempted our Lord to become his heir rather than the heir of God, his heavenly Father.

In reading Eve's reply to the devil, notice that she knew that God had treated both she and her husband as one (or one party of a covenant) when He gave them the command regarding the tree of the knowledge of good and evil, and the provision and promise of life, even life eternal.

Now, during the interaction between Eve and the serpent, Adam was present but did not intervene. He failed to assume his place of authority and responsibility to exercise counsel, wisdom, or judgment over a matter that was his duty to safeguard and judge (Luke 3:37; Galatians 3:26–29). Why he did nothing is easy to discern. Being tempted himself and falling into the weakness of his own flesh, he could not resist the urge to touch what was unknown and desirable. (A similar story is recorded of the evil royal family of Ahab and Jezebel, which was another example God used in human history to teach us about spiritual position and divine order—with these, spiritual responsibility and obedience.)

A side note: It is quite sobering when we consider this in the light of contemporary Christianity and the secular world today. How many people are being tempted by supernatural power and spiritual mysteries and are lured into false religion, idol worship, spiritual mysticism, witchcraft, fortune-telling, mediums, etc.? All the while, they remain ignorant of the fact that these are the very kinds of spiritual foods of which God would never want man to partake.

Second, Satan imputed doubt into man's mind regarding the truthfulness and faithfulness of God and His willingness and power to protect him.

In essence, Satan was communicating that God could not be trusted, so man would have to trust in himself—in his own wisdom and ability.

God's verdict for those who choose to eat from the tree of the knowledge of good and evil, or partake of a wisdom that is not from Him, is this: "You will surely die." Oh! How subtle are the ways of the devil! You see, when Satan said to Eve, "You will not surely die." He challenged the judgment of God concerning His sovereignty, as if there are things that God did not know and could not control. The devil also challenged God's goodness, as if He would withhold good things from man. The truth, however, is that God intends for man to fully know Him even as he is known. In this intimate relationship, God would withhold nothing from him in terms of His goodness, His wisdom, His power, and even His honor and glory. He will give man all things as a beloved son and blessed heir. Even so, on a son's part, obedience is required to receive such a rich inheritance.

Now, compare this to Jesus in the desert: When the devil tempted Jesus to throw himself down from the pinnacle of the temple, Jesus was facing a test of a similar nature. That is, God's judgment and power concerning death and life. Notice, in this test, it is not so much a matter of whether or not the help of angels would be available to Jesus. That is, would God his Father fail to fulfill His word or promise concerning His son? Rather, it was more of a matter of his faith in his Father's judgment. That is, would a son distrust God his Father and venture into something outside of His counsel and instruction? An obedient son of God will not test or tempt the heavenly Father, because that would only happen when his heart is not in the right place. No, the true son will, with trust, learn to obey the Father in all things. How foolish then are those who will throw away all restraint and put God to the test? They may not question His goodness, but they will question His judgment—not knowing that His judgment embodies His justice, righteousness, and truthfulness. They would dare to provoke God to anger, even to the point of having to demonstrate His power in judgment or wrath.

Disobedience is, by nature, divination, as Samuel rightfully put it, for it is to test God (1 Samuel 15). The apostle John said that sin is lawlessness, which is the doorway for the lawless one or the antichrist to work through the disobedience of man (1 John 3:4). Why? Because sin, in such a context, is to distrust God's character, which is His goodness and love issued from His divine nature. To distrust His ways, which are His righteousness and justice, upheld by His authority and power. Such a sinful or unbelieving heart naturally makes God's love and grace "powerless." Repentance is the only way out of it.

The third temptation is related to our glory or perfection in God, or the true purpose of human existence.

The devil challenged Eve with two things: 1) whether or not God has man's best in mind. 2) whether or not He knows how to accomplish it. Eve fell into the second trap. She acknowledged the goodness of God when she stated that man had not been forbidden to eat any of the fruit in the garden, either natural or spiritual (the tree of life), except one, the tree of knowledge of good and evil—which would induce the judgment of death. However, she was tempted to believe, at the persuasion of the devil, that somehow, she could find her own way to gain wisdom and become like God, by distrusting His goodness and disobeying His strict command. Adam did the same when he became a partner in Eve's sin. In contrast, however, Jesus did not fall into this sin. Never had he asked for any false glory, nor ever attempted to attain God's promise by his own means. Even when the devil conveniently offered it to him, seemingly without any "real cost," Jesus refused to bow and worship the devil (John 5:41–44, John 8:27–29, John 8:31–59). Later, he readily shared with his disciples this truth: "What good is it for a man to gain the whole world by having forfeited his own soul?" Surely, Jesus knew what was at stake.

Today, cultural relevance, social pragmatism, and secular humanism (which serve man's interests rather than God's) have permeated the diverse streams of wisdom, religion and philosophy in the world. In the guise of God's goodness and the brotherhood of man, they have even infiltrated the ranks of Christianity with all kinds of doctrines and practices. It is sad to witness that the yeast of modern Pharisees and Sadducees subtly finds its way into the forums and pulpits of God's people. With such a deluge of deception, it is difficult to stand firm, remaining untainted and uncompromising in God's pure truth and holiness, and commit ourselves totally to Him for our wellbeing and for the values of life. A thick veil is covering the minds of many—keeping them from being able to trust, hear, and obey God. Many invisible chains and yolks forged by the deceptive ways of the evil one are enslaving and oppressing the very people who are eagerly seeking God, and are willing to serve Him with a genuine and devout heart. How sad!

> "A people, with a pure heart and a holy passion are eagerly and diligently seeking to truly know and represent their Father in Heaven, and to go about His business on earth with His divine wisdom and empowerment."

But, glory to God, a holy remnant is now rising up from the rubbles and ruins of man's futility and vanity. A people, with a pure heart and a holy passion are eagerly and diligently seeking to truly know and represent their Father in Heaven, and to go about His business on earth with His divine wisdom and empowerment.

We are witnessing, in this unique "day" of mankind, a light shining forth brilliantly from the thick darkness. Even now, more darkness is being unleashed and its attempt to cover over this dying and hopeless world is being intensified. But, God is forging a strong and faithful people to make a difference. Indeed, when evil comes like a flood, God will raise up a holy standard, so that His knowledge and glory will break out from all darkness and cover the earth like the waters cover the sea. Has He not promised us this day in His word? Now, His day is coming!

Consequences of the Fall

The consequences of man's fall are severe and grievous. Here are a few:

> 1. Man lost the privilege to fellowship with God (who is Spirit) and with it, he lost the opportunity to learn wisdom and love from Him. Much of man's initial capacity for spiritual life and understanding was shut down when the Spirit of sonship was taken away. This means that man would no longer be able to communicate with God in the way He had originally intended for him, which is to fellowship with him as a father would with his son. Through this relationship, He would teach His sons all things and have His sons grow up to be just like Him. The divine process of producing sons of God through the human race and transforming man into His spiritual offspring was cut off.

> 2. Man lost the authority and privilege to represent God to creation and to rule over it, which is to impart His wisdom,

glory, and love. We lost our position as kings and priests in His Kingdom and Household. By His original design, in kingship, we would rule with righteousness on God's behalf as His sons. He Himself would be the Judge of all judges and the King of all kings. In priesthood, we would act as ministers or servants of a covenant of eternal life between God and those who are to learn of Him—to the whole of creation. This service is in order to impute His wisdom, order, peace, and love to them, and to teach them His goodness, holiness, righteousness, and faithfulness.

3. Man lost power over the devil, and thus over the angelic realm and the earthly realm. He was weakened and for the most part, became powerless to withstand the evil one's schemes and assaults. The devil usurped our dominion over God's creation, both in the angelic realm as well as in the earthly realm. The world (this creation or this age) was thus caught up in a war between the Kingdom of Darkness and the Kingdom of God and His Christ. Only in Christ Jesus are we freed from the terror of the evil one and the fear of death. In this sense, we also lost our protection in God as sons of Adam. We, as sons of Adam, became slaves of sin and death, victims of evil and deception.

4. Man lost the blessing of God's provision, physical as well as spiritual. He had no access to the substance of spiritual life in God anymore. More so, as a punishment for sin and disbelief, and as a reminder of his miserable state and powerless position, God made man labor by the sweat of his brow, as a lowly creature just to sustain his earthly life in a cursed world. From the moment that he is born into this world, he is in corruption. All the while,

the everlasting call of the Father was for man to return to his spiritual home. Woman is to suffer pain in childbirth, symbolizing man's fate of suffering until death. That is, he is to be born with suffering and pain, only to return to dust without a trace. How sad is the Fall of man, and how miserable his end! In sin and unto death he toils in a cursed world and groans inside, never able to be truly free.

5. Man lost eternal life in God. Mankind was doomed, along with all creation, to decay and to perish in the end. The tree of life was out of man's reach after he was cast out of the Garden. It was guarded by water and fire, by cherubim with fiery swords to execute the judgment of death. Can you imagine how sad it would be for us to be cast away from our earthly father and mother, and our home where our family gathers together? Yet man, as a race, was cast away from his family in heaven and from the purest form of life and love, which had promised to be abundant and most fulfilling, even a life filled with the very glory and blessedness of God.

6. Man lost peace, love, and righteousness in life. As we can see, because of sin and shame, Adam began to blame Eve, and Eve turned around to blame the serpent. The tragedy continued. Their firstborn child, Cain, killed his brother, Abel, out of jealousy. Blood was shed between brothers and within a family. For the first time, innocent blood and death were tasted by the very soil that should have been the seedbed of life, peace, and happiness. Sin quickly brought about the degradation of man's heart towards his fellow beings. Had Christ not come, war and death would never withdraw themselves from the fate of

mankind until his flesh is taken away and the creation is wrapped up.

7. Man lost many abilities to create, to gain wisdom and understanding, and to love as God would love. Even the natural faculties of our being were locked up. Man's span of life was shortened. Disease and pain began to inflict mankind. Man was now to witness and to be afflicted by all forms of sickness, wickedness, sorrow, and suffering. In a sense, man became a miserable creation, burning with a sense of loss and dissatisfaction as his faculties of love and understanding were locked up by his lowly form of life, marred by his selfish desires and sinful cravings.

Without God, we are doomed. Without God, we are lost. Without God, we are living beings of lack. Without God, we are creatures of misery. From dust we come, and to dust we return. We perish like grass. We wither like a flower. We are carried off as in a flood. We are gone as with the wind.

SCRIPTURES

The Fall

ROMANS 5:12-14

¹² Therefore, just as sin entered the world through one man, and death through sin, and in this way death came to all men, because all sinned— ¹³ for before the law was given, sin was in the world. But sin is not taken into account when there is no law. ¹⁴ Nevertheless, death reigned from the time of Adam to the time of Moses, even over those who did not sin by breaking a command, as did Adam, who was a pattern of the one to come.

1 CORINTHIANS 15:45-49

⁴⁵ So it is written: "The first man Adam became a living being"; the last Adam, a life-giving spirit. ⁴⁶ The spiritual did not come first, but the natural, and after that the spiritual. ⁴⁷ The first man was of the dust of the earth, the second man from heaven. ⁴⁸ As was the earthly man, so are those who are of the earth; and as is the man from heaven, so also are those who are of heaven. ⁴⁹ And just as we have borne the likeness of the earthly man, so shall we bear the likeness of the man from heaven.

1 CORINTHIANS 11:3

³ Now I want you to realize that the head of every man is Christ, and the head of the woman is man, and the head of Christ is God.

1 CORINTHIANS 11:7-10

⁷ A man ought not to cover his head, since he is the image and glory of God; but the woman is the glory of man. ⁸ For man did not come from woman, but woman from man; ⁹ neither was man created for woman, but woman for man. ¹⁰ For this reason, and because of the angels, the woman ought to have a sign of authority on her head.

On Temptation

1 CORINTHIANS 10:13
¹³ No temptation has seized you except what is common to man. And God is faithful; he will not let you be tempted beyond what you can bear. But when you are tempted, he will also provide a way out so that you can stand up under it.

JAMES 1:13–15
¹³ When tempted, no one should say, "God is tempting me." For God cannot be tempted by evil, nor does he tempt anyone; ¹⁴ but each one is tempted when, by his own evil desire, he is dragged away and enticed. ¹⁵ Then, after desire has conceived, it gives birth to sin; and sin, when it is full-grown, gives birth to death.

2 CORINTHIANS 2:9
⁹ The reason I wrote you was to see if you would stand the test and be obedient in everything.

HEBREWS 4:15–16
¹⁵ For we do not have a high priest who is unable to sympathize with our weaknesses, but we have one who has been tempted in every way, just as we are—yet was without sin. ¹⁶ Let us then approach the throne of grace with confidence, so that we may receive mercy and find grace to help us in our time of need.

GALATIANS 6:1–2
¹ Brothers, if someone is caught in a sin, you who are spiritual should restore him gently. But watch yourself, or you also may be tempted. ² Carry each other's burdens, and in this way you will fulfill the law of Christ.

On Overcoming

LUKE 10:19
¹⁹ I have given you authority to trample on snakes and scorpions and to overcome all the power of the enemy; nothing will harm you.

1 JOHN 5:3-5
³ This is love for God: to obey his commands. And his commands are not burdensome, ⁴ for everyone born of God overcomes the world. This is the victory that has overcome the world, even our faith. ⁵ Who is it that overcomes the world? Only he who believes that Jesus is the Son of God.

REVELATION 2:7
⁷ He who has an ear, let him hear what the Spirit says to the churches. To him who overcomes, I will give the right to eat from the tree of life, which is in the paradise of God.

REVELATION 2:11
¹¹ He who has an ear, let him hear what the Spirit says to the churches. He who overcomes will not be hurt at all by the second death

REVELATION 2:17
¹⁷ He who has an ear, let him hear what the Spirit says to the churches. To him who overcomes, I will give some of the hidden manna. I will also give him a white stone with a new name written on it, known only to him who receives it.

REVELATION 2:26-28
²⁶ To him who overcomes and does my will to the end, I will give authority over the nations— ²⁷ 'He will rule them with an iron scepter; he will dash them to pieces like pottery'— just as I have received authority from my Father. ²⁸ I will also give him the morning star.

REVELATION 3:5

⁵ *He who overcomes will, like them, be dressed in white. I will never blot out his name from the book of life, but will acknowledge his name before my Father and his angels.*

REVELATION 3:12

¹² *Him who overcomes I will make a pillar in the temple of my God. Never again will he leave it. I will write on him the name of my God and the name of the city of my God, the new Jerusalem, which is coming down out of heaven from my God; and I will also write on him my new name.*

REVELATION 3:21

²¹ *To him who overcomes, I will give the right to sit with me on my throne, just as I overcame and sat down with my Father on his throne.*

REVELATION 21:3–8

³ *And I heard a loud voice from the throne saying, "Now the dwelling of God is with men, and he will live with them. They will be his people, and God himself will be with them and be their God.* ⁴ *He will wipe every tear from their eyes. There will be no more death or mourning or crying or pain, for the old order of things has passed away."*
⁵ *He who was seated on the throne said, "I am making everything new!" Then he said, "Write this down, for these words are trustworthy and true."*
⁶ *He said to me: "It is done. I am the Alpha and the Omega, the Beginning and the End. To him who is thirsty I will give to drink without cost from the spring of the water of life.* ⁷ *He who overcomes will inherit all this, and I will be his God and he will be my son.*
⁸ *But the cowardly, the unbelieving, the vile, the murderers, the sexually immoral, those who practice magic arts, the idolaters and all liars—their place will be in the fiery lake of burning sulfur. This is the second death."*

QUESTIONS FOR REVIEW

1. What stands out to you as you consider the Fall of man and its consequences?

2. Read the following verse. In what way do you think this correlates to the temptations that Adam and Jesus faced?

1 JOHN 2:15–17

^{15} Do not love the world or anything in the world. If anyone loves the world, the love of the Father is not in him. ^{16} For everything in the world—the cravings of sinful man, the lust of his eyes and the boasting of what he has and does—comes not from the Father but from the world. ^{17} The world and its desires pass away, but the man who does the will of God lives forever.

3. In what ways are the temptations of Adam and Eve similar to those of Jesus? Are there any differences?

_____

_____

_____

4. Out of the seven points regarding the Fall of man listed above, name two that you deem as major in your life. How and why?

_____

_____

_____

QUESTIONS
FOR MEDITATION & APPLICATION

1. All men sin and are prone to fall into temptation because of the Adamic nature. What are the worst temptations you are facing today?

_____

_____

_____

- Why should you overcome them?

_____

_____

- How can you overcome them?

_____

_____

4

THE CROSS

OVERVIEW

In this chapter, we will survey the cross where Jesus Christ, the Son of Man and the Son of God, died and took away the sin of the world.

- The Tree of Knowledge of Good and Evil versus the Tree of Life

- The Cross:

    - Curse and Blessing

    - Death and Life

    - Sin and Forgiveness

- The reconciliation of man and the restoration of all things

In the last chapter, we visited the Fall of man and the grievous consequences that were inflicted upon mankind. Through one man sin entered the world, and death began to dominate the whole world. Not only was the race of man "bitten in the heel" by the serpent, but the poison of death also spread to all creation. Through the power of death and the dominion of hades, the devil became the ruler of this world (age)—ruling over the living and the dead. He is the prince of the air, the accuser of mankind, the head of all rebellious spirits and dominions, and the tormentor of man's soul and flesh. War, famine, disease, and all forms of wickedness and evil, devastating and terrifying, began to permeate the creation that God had allotted to man for his happiness. Man became a victim of lust, sin, and death. He became the pawn of the evil one and his agents. Man is powerless, defenseless, hopeless, and helpless in the face of his unbridled depravity, cruelty, and thirst for the blood of even his own brethren. He becomes the prey and plunder of the evil one under the sway of all his schemes and attacks.

Man becomes a creature without rest and without hope. What happened? Even with the best of his knowledge and intelligence, through endless endeavors and persistent efforts, he couldn't even get close to a culture of love, peace, and goodness. If there is no escape from the curse of the Fall, then what would be the end of this fatal disease? Where is our hope?

Again, let's turn to the "beginning" to find the answer.

TWO TREES

In the beginning, God put two trees in the middle of the Garden of Eden: the tree of the knowledge of good and evil, and the tree of life.

The Tree of Death

He commanded Adam and Eve to not eat from the tree of the knowledge of good and evil, or they would surely die. So, we could call this tree, "the tree of death." But He did not deny their access to the tree of life until they had disobeyed.

> **GENESIS 3:4-6**
> *[4] "You will not surely die," the serpent said to the woman. [5] "For God knows that when you eat of it your eyes will be opened, and you will be like God, knowing good and evil."*
> *[6] When the woman saw that the fruit of the tree was good for food and pleasing to the eye, and also desirable for gaining wisdom, she took some and ate it. She also gave some to her husband, who was with her, and he ate it.*

Let's make some observations about what happened here in Genesis and look at the results of eating the "forbidden fruit."

What "Eyes" were Opened?

In the previous chapter, we discussed the many tactics and temptations used by the serpent to convince Eve and Adam to partake of the fruit from the tree of death. One in particular had to do with the lust of man in coveting God's wisdom in a wrong way. This was described by Paul as the way of the flesh or the carnal mind. The "eyes" that were opened were the eyes of the flesh, the gateway through which they were plunged into a natural world void of spiritual light.

Before this "eye opening", even though they were flesh and blood, man had the Holy Spirit interacting with his spirit. The human spirit counseled his own soul in an orderly and flawless way and reigned over his own flesh. The heart of man flowed freely with the counsel of God. The result was that his thoughts (mind) and actions (body) in his soul and his physical life were in perfect alignment with God's wisdom and will. There was no separation between the three compartments of man as a living being. His spirit, soul, and body were fully within the life and counsel that God intended for them. Although they were not yet mature in God, through their free and loving fellowship with Him, they were to be made like Him in every way. Indeed, it would be the great pleasure of God to be their Father and give them His very life, along with everything that He has.

However, when Adam and Eve ate the fruit from the tree of the knowledge of good and evil, their eyes were opened to the natural world and to a wisdom that was alien to the one God had intended for them. This base and earthly wisdom began to defile their conscience and their way of thinking. Their life would now be confined by a visible reality, and that being the self-consciousness in the mind. Lacking God's fellowship, and thus His provision, protection, and wisdom, they were compelled to conduct their life by giving priority to "self," and therefore under the whim of the evil one. This is the nature of what Jesus and the early apostles referred to as "lawlessness" (being void of the order of God's life) or "sin" (missing the mark or the purpose for which they were created, and what they were endowed with from the time they were created).

The true knowledge of God would not be illuminated to them through this base and false wisdom. The knowledge of God (of His person, and His ways) can only be approached and understood by a spiritual being with spiritual consciousness and spiritual faculties. God is Spirit. His Kingdom or domain is a spiritual and eternal reality, above and beyond the visible and temporal world that man was cast into and in which he is caged. In terms of spiritual truth, man was now in total darkness. He began to subvert his ability to learn, create, and manage things for his own wellbeing to a point of depravity and to take pride in his own wisdom and achievements.

This is why Paul would say that no flesh and blood can enter the Kingdom of God. Jesus said that a man's flesh will always war against the spirit. These statements are not merely about our struggles against the power of sin or the evil desires within. Rather, they are pointing to a bigger reality which was designed to be veiled from man's intellect, or his carnal mind. Man's knowledge, reasoning, and imagination had come to a lowly state—based on a lowly reality and a culture of disarray, without order, love, or understanding from God. This was the core of the sin of man. He was doomed to "miss the mark" of having real life in God.

How Sin Leads to Death and Lawlessness

One important thing we need to recognize is that there is a spiritual position and a kingdom responsibility that God only gives to His mature sons in whom He is well pleased. Only these would be entrusted with the role and responsibility to represent Him to all creation with righteousness and justice. They are to mediate, under the headship (leadership) of Christ, on behalf of what is created, before God the Father and the Lord Jesus Christ with the love, wisdom, and mercy God the Father intends to embody and dispense through them as sons. Later, we will expound more on this spiritual order and its ministry that exists in the realm of God, which is the Order of Melchizedek. Sadly, through the Fall, Man's freewill, a unique gift given to him by God to receive and offer love, was, through the deception of the serpent, usurped to partake, manage, and even create things outside of God's will and against His nature—which is righteousness, holiness, love, and goodness.

Having exercised this freewill in the partaking of "the forbidden fruit" (a false wisdom), man began to entertain and produce his own concept and standard of justice and judgment. This was rooted in the pride of having by himself the right and the ability to decide what is right and what is wrong. The goal of man's judgment then was to strive for his wellbeing by his own means.

Man began to take justice in his own hands. First, he formed his own standard of righteousness and justice. Second, he began to muster his strength or power to obtain them. This was evident in the life of Cain. He made his brother Abel his enemy and killed him because sin entered into his mind. He did it for two obvious reasons. First, because Abel seemed to enjoy a better place before God, so Cain felt he was put into a position of injustice and was being mistreated by God. Second, against God's warning and counsel, he allowed sin to enter his heart and mind, and yielded to the demonic desire to avenge himself. Yet Abel was his brother, and was supposed to be the target of his love and support instead of hatred and competition.

Here we see a pattern: disobedience leads to sin, sin leads to death, and death leads to the violation of God's way of love. The result is broken human relationships. This is against the constitution that God had designed for the family of man—righteousness, peace, and love in the Holy Spirit; a life of love unto God and one another.

We can also see that the partaking of this bad fruit gave man a false counsel. Right as it may seem in his own eyes, it opened the door for sin and lawlessness to enter and rule the world.

Unfortunately, this was not just man's own making. It was caused by the enemy of God, our adversary, the devil. And he is also the one presiding over such powers, the one who truly rules the world.

The Poison of Man's Conscience

When Adam and Eve's eyes were opened to this wisdom (which is "from below" and only by their earthly nature) they lost what Paul would call "a clean conscience." They began to be assaulted by all kinds of wrong things.

> 1. They began to have shame. Nakedness was revealed to man and creation, so they tried to veil or cover it, first using fig leaves. Later God made garments of animal skin to clothe them. They came to their shame, or sense of

unrighteousness, recognizing that they were not worthy to stand in the presence of God, not to mention be able to represent Him. From that day on, the shame of sin began to torment man.

2. They began to have <u>fear</u>. The spirit of fear is in opposition with the Spirit of sonship as explained by Paul (Romans 8:13-15). Fear is the outcome of an awareness of God's justice and righteousness and our own wretchedness. Without a mediator, man would have to face the consequences of his sin before God. Due to the lack of understanding of God's goodness, man could not apprehend the concept of forgiveness, nor did he have the means to attain it. Adam and Eve had to hide from God's presence where His love, counsel, life, and glory preside. The consequence of sin and disobedience was and is death. From that day on, the fear of death began to assault man.

Now we can see, this bad tree is where the curse or judgment of God is issued. It was as if Adam and Eve had hung themselves on this tree and never got off of it, and with them are those who are born of them as their descendants—the sons of Adam.

The Tree of Life

Genesis does not offer us a clear picture of the tree of life. We know that it stands beside the tree of death in the center of four rivers (streams). That means that these two trees were equally accessible to man. Later God had to cast Adam and Eve out of the Garden of Eden in order to deny their access to it.

GENESIS 3:22-24

²² *And the Lord God said, "The man has now become like one of us, knowing good and evil. He must not be allowed to reach out his hand and take also from the tree of life and eat, and live forever."* ²³ *So the Lord God banished him from the Garden of Eden to work the ground from which he had been taken.* ²⁴ *After he drove the man out, he placed on the east side of the Garden of Eden cherubim and a flaming sword flashing back and forth to guard the way to the tree of life.*

Here are some brief observations of the above verses.

"Man became like one of us." In this likeness to God, the fullness of His nature is not implied. Judgment, or the knowing of good and evil, is only one attribute of God's whole nature and character. The knowledge of good and evil alone could never produce His wisdom, especially when deprived of His love. This would be like a son who is given the privilege and role of representing his father, who would then spurn the goodness of his father in an act of rebellion, defaming his father and forfeiting his birthright which had promised a rich inheritance. He did not add honor and pleasure to his father (becoming his joy and satisfaction), so the glory and pride of his father were not attained. Rather, in rebellion, he brought dishonor, pain, and sorrow to his father. What else could the father do but to take away his inheritance and cast him out of the family? That is exactly what happened to Adam and Eve in the beginning. They were cast out of God's Family. They forfeited their sonship in Him. With no access to the tree of life, they were denied eternal life, which was part of their inheritance from God the Father as a son.

However, we know that this is the very tree whose fruits God desires man to partake of, so that he could have eternal life and fellowship with Him as a family.

THE CROSS

The picture of death and the judgment of a rebellious son are expressed in the law God gave to Moses in Deuteronomy 21:18–23, "Cursed is anyone who is hung on a tree."

Commenting on this, Paul explained:

> **GALATIANS 3:7–14**
> *⁷ Understand, then, that those who believe are children of Abraham. ⁸ The Scripture foresaw that God would justify the Gentiles by faith, and announced the gospel in advance to Abraham: "All nations will be blessed through you." ⁹ So those who have faith are blessed along with Abraham, the man of faith.*
> *¹⁰ All who rely on observing the law are under a curse, for it is written: "Cursed is everyone who does not continue to do everything written in the Book of the Law." ¹¹ Clearly no one is justified before God by the law, because, "The righteous will live by faith." ¹² The law is not based on faith; on the contrary, "The man who does these things will live by them." ¹³ Christ redeemed us from the curse of the law by becoming a curse for us, for it is written: "Cursed is everyone who is hung on a tree." ¹⁴ He redeemed us in order that the blessing given to Abraham might come to the Gentiles through Christ Jesus, so that by faith we might receive the promise of the Spirit.*

"Dust you are and to dust you will return," (Genesis 3:19). But through the death of Jesus Christ on the cross, we are saved from this tragic fate. Paul expounded on this in the book of Romans.

> **ROMANS 5:6–21**
> *⁶ You see, at just the right time, when we were still powerless, Christ died for the ungodly. ⁷ Very rarely will anyone die for a righteous man, though for a good man someone might possibly dare to die. ⁸ But God demonstrates his own love for us in this: While we were still sinners, Christ died for us. ⁹ Since we have now been justified by his blood, how much more shall we be saved from God's wrath through him! ¹⁰ For if, when we were God's enemies, we were reconciled to him through the death of his Son, how much more, having been reconciled, shall we be saved through his life! ¹¹ Not only is this so, but we also rejoice in God through our Lord Jesus Christ, through whom we have now received reconciliation.*
>
> *¹² Therefore, just as sin entered the world through one man, and death through sin, and in this way death came to all men, because all sinned—*
> *¹³ for before the law was given, sin was in the world. But sin is not taken into account when there is no law. ¹⁴ Nevertheless, death reigned from the time of Adam to the time of Moses, even over those who did not sin by breaking a command, as did Adam, who was a pattern of the one to come.*
> *¹⁵ But the gift is not like the trespass. For if the many died by the trespass of the one man, how much more did God's grace and the gift that came by the grace of the one man, Jesus Christ, overflow to the many! ¹⁶ Again, the gift of God is not like the result of the one man's sin: The judgment followed one sin and brought condemnation, but the gift followed many trespasses and brought justification. ¹⁷ For if, by the trespass of the one man, death reigned*

The Cross

> *through that one man, how much more will those who receive God's abundant provision of grace and of the gift of righteousness reign in life through the one man, Jesus Christ. ¹⁸ Consequently, just as the result of one trespass was condemnation for all men, so also the result of one act of righteousness was justification that brings life for all men. ¹⁹ For just as through the disobedience of the one man the many were made sinners, so also through the obedience of the one man the many will be made righteous.*
> *²⁰ The law was added so that the trespass might increase. But where sin increased, grace increased all the more, ²¹ so that, just as sin reigned in death, so also grace might reign through righteousness to bring eternal life through Jesus Christ our Lord.*

To those who put their faith in Christ Jesus, they will receive the full benefit of the cross. What are these benefits? Let's first look at the symbolic meaning of the cross.

The cross represents the "two trees" together: 1) the death of Christ Jesus in our stead and 2) eternal life in the Father through Him.

ROMANS 6:8-10
> *⁸ Now if we died with Christ, we believe that we will also live with him. ⁹ For we know that since Christ was raised from the dead, he cannot die again; death no longer has mastery over him. ¹⁰ The death he died, he died to sin once for all; but the life he lives, he lives to God.*

By identifying himself as a man and willingly becoming the embodiment of sin, Jesus took on the full wrath of God. He canceled the curse of sin and death unto man once and for all and became the way to eternal life. Through the atoning power of his blood, we are reconciled back to God the Father. And He freely gives us the Spirit of sonship.

ROMANS 8:1-17

[1] Therefore, there is now no condemnation for those who are in Christ Jesus, [2] because through Christ Jesus the law of the Spirit of life set me free from the law of sin and death. [3] For what the law was powerless to do in that it was weakened by the sinful nature, God did by sending his own Son in the likeness of sinful man to be a sin offering. And so he condemned sin in sinful man, [4] in order that the righteous requirements of the law might be fully met in us, who do not live according to the sinful nature but according to the Spirit.

[5] Those who live according to the sinful nature have their minds set on what that nature desires; but those who live in accordance with the Spirit have their minds set on what the Spirit desires. [6] The mind of sinful man is death, but the mind controlled by the Spirit is life and peace; [7] the sinful mind is hostile to God. It does not submit to God's law, nor can it do so. [8] Those controlled by the sinful nature cannot please God.

[9] You, however, are controlled not by the sinful nature but by the Spirit, if the Spirit of God lives in you. And if anyone does not have the Spirit of Christ, he does not belong to Christ. [10] But if Christ is in you, your body is dead because of sin, yet your spirit is alive because of righteousness. [11] And if the Spirit of him who raised Jesus from the dead is living in you, he who raised Christ from the dead will also give life to your mortal bodies through his Spirit, who lives in you.

[12] Therefore, brothers, we have an obligation—but it is not to the sinful nature, to live according to it. [13] For if you live according to the sinful nature, you will die; but if by the Spirit you put to death

the misdeeds of the body, you will live,
¹⁴ because those who are led by the Spirit of God are sons of God.
¹⁵ For you did not receive a spirit that makes you a slave again to fear, but you received the Spirit of sonship. And by him we cry, "Abba, Father." ¹⁶ The Spirit himself testifies with our spirit that we are God's children. ¹⁷ Now if we are children, then we are heirs—heirs of God and co-heirs with Christ, if indeed we share in his sufferings in order that we may also share in his glory.

THE RECONCILIATION OF MAN AND THE RESTITUTION OF ALL THINGS

With a brief review of what man suffered in the Fall, we can see how much Christ has restored to us through his death, burial, resurrection, and ascension. We are more than being reconciled back to God, the entirety of His sovereign will and purpose for us has been restored back to us. We also have the Son himself as our brother, our friend, our High Priest and Mediator, and our Lord and King who will always intercede before the Father on our behalf as we put our faith in him and walk in his Spirit. We are kept immune to the power and afflictions of sin and death. We are clothed with his power, life, and glory in all righteousness. We are made holy as he is holy, and sons of God even as he is the Son of God.

HEBREWS 2:9-11

⁹ But we see Jesus, who was made a little lower than the angels, now crowned with glory and honor because he suffered death, so that by the grace of God he might taste death for everyone.

> *¹⁰ In bringing many sons to glory, it was fitting that God, for whom and through whom everything exists, should make the author of their salvation perfect through suffering. ¹¹ Both the one who makes men holy and those who are made holy are of the same family. So Jesus is not ashamed to call them brothers.*

We are now sons of God with access to the tree of life. When we partake of its fruits, we will have eternal life in God. What kind of fruits are these? In short, they are none other than the true wisdom of God, preserved to be partaken by His sons only. Notice that Adam and Eve were ignorant of its value, and never partook of any fruits from this tree. In essence, they never truly understood the Father's desire and intention for planting the tree of life in the garden. Thus, in a sense, they were like Esau who never had the right attitude and understanding of what God wanted for them, and for their own true good. They despised the birthright and the inheritance of eternal life as a son of God.

> **"We are more than being reconciled back to God, the entirety of His sovereign will and purpose for us has been restored back to us."**

But, in Christ Jesus, this is fully restored to us! Because of this truth and revelation, Paul exclaimed it with great excitement and joy in many of his epistles.

1 CORINTHIANS 15:54–57

⁵⁴ *When the perishable has been clothed with the imperishable, and the mortal with immortality, then the saying that is written will come true: "Death has been swallowed up in victory."*
⁵⁵ *"Where, O death, is your victory? Where, O death, is your sting?"*
⁵⁶ *The sting of death is sin, and the power of sin is the law.* ⁵⁷ *But thanks be to God! He gives us the victory through our Lord Jesus Christ.*

ROMANS 8:31–39

³¹ *What, then, shall we say in response to this? If God is for us, who can be against us?* ³² *He who did not spare his own Son, but gave him up for us all—how will he not also, along with him, graciously give us all things?* ³³ *Who will bring any charge against those whom God has chosen? It is God who justifies.* ³⁴ *Who is he that condemns? Christ Jesus, who died—more than that, who was raised to life—is at the right hand of God and is also interceding for us.* ³⁵ *Who shall separate us from the love of Christ? Shall trouble or hardship or persecution or famine or nakedness or danger or sword?* ³⁶ *As it is written:*
"For your sake we face death all day long; we are considered as sheep to be slaughtered."
³⁷ *No, in all these things we are more than conquerors through him who loved us.* ³⁸ *For I am convinced that neither death nor life, neither angels nor demons, neither the present nor the future, nor any powers,* ³⁹ *neither height nor depth, nor anything else in all creation, will be able to separate us from the love of God that is in Christ Jesus our Lord.*

ROMANS 11:33–36

³³ *Oh, the depth of the riches of the wisdom and knowledge of God! How unsearchable his judgments, and his paths beyond tracing out!*

³⁴ "Who has known the mind of the Lord? Or who has been his counselor?"
³⁵ "Who has ever given to God, that God should repay him?"
³⁶ For from him and through him and to him are all things. To him be the glory forever! Amen.

SCRIPTURES

We have already included many scriptures in this chapter. Please review those carefully before continuing.

Two Trees

PSALM 1:1-3
¹ Blessed is the man
who does not walk in the counsel of the wicked
or stand in the way of sinners
or sit in the seat of mockers.
² But his delight is in the law of the Lord,
and on his law he meditates day and night.
³ He is like a tree planted by streams of water,
which yields its fruit in season
and whose leaf does not wither.
Whatever he does prospers.

ISAIAH 6:13
¹³ And though a tenth remains in the land, it will again be laid waste. But as the terebinth and oak leave stumps when they are cut down, so the holy seed will be the stump in the land."

ISAIAH 11:1
¹ A shoot will come up from the stump of Jesse; from his roots a Branch will bear fruit.

MATTHEW 13:31-32
³¹ He told them another parable: "The kingdom of heaven is like a mustard seed, which a man took and planted in his field. ³² Though it

is the smallest of all your seeds, yet when it grows, it is the largest of garden plants and becomes a tree, so that the birds of the air come and perch in its branches."

REVELATION 22:1–5

¹ Then the angel showed me the river of the water of life, as clear as crystal, flowing from the throne of God and of the Lamb ² down the middle of the great street of the city. On each side of the river stood the tree of life, bearing twelve crops of fruit, yielding its fruit every month. And the leaves of the tree are for the healing of the nations. ³ No longer will there be any curse. The throne of God and of the Lamb will be in the city, and his servants will serve him. ⁴ They will see his face, and his name will be on their foreheads. ⁵ There will be no more night. They will not need the light of a lamp or the light of the sun, for the Lord God will give them light. And they will reign for ever and ever.

The Cross

NUMBERS 21:4–9

⁴ They traveled from Mount Hor along the route to the Red Sea, to go around Edom. But the people grew impatient on the way; ⁵ they spoke against God and against Moses, and said, "Why have you brought us up out of Egypt to die in the desert? There is no bread! There is no water! And we detest this miserable food!"

⁶ Then the Lord sent venomous snakes among them; they bit the people and many Israelites died. ⁷ The people came to Moses and said, "We sinned when we spoke against the Lord and against you. Pray that the Lord will take the snakes away from us." So Moses prayed for the people.

⁸ The Lord said to Moses, "Make a snake and put it up on a pole; anyone who is bitten can look at it and live." ⁹ So Moses made a bronze snake and put it up on a pole. Then when anyone was bitten by a snake and looked at the bronze snake, he lived.

JOHN 3:10–18

[10] "You are Israel's teacher," said Jesus, "and do you not understand these things? [11] I tell you the truth, we speak of what we know, and we testify to what we have seen, but still you people do not accept our testimony. [12] I have spoken to you of earthly things and you do not believe; how then will you believe if I speak of heavenly things? [13] No one has ever gone into heaven except the one who came from heaven—the Son of Man. [14] Just as Moses lifted up the snake in the desert, so the Son of Man must be lifted up, [15] that everyone who believes in him may have eternal life

[16] "For God so loved the world that he gave his one and only Son, that whoever believes in him shall not perish but have eternal life. [17] For God did not send his Son into the world to condemn the world, but to save the world through him. [18] Whoever believes in him is not condemned, but whoever does not believe stands condemned already because he has not believed in the name of God's one and only Son.

JOHN 12:23–36

[23] Jesus replied, "The hour has come for the Son of Man to be glorified. [24] I tell you the truth, unless a kernel of wheat falls to the ground and dies, it remains only a single seed. But if it dies, it produces many seeds. [25] The man who loves his life will lose it, while the man who hates his life in this world will keep it for eternal life. [26] Whoever serves me must follow me; and where I am, my servant also will be. My Father will honor the one who serves me.

[27] "Now my heart is troubled, and what shall I say? 'Father, save me from this hour'? No, it was for this very reason I came to this hour. [28] Father, glorify your name!" Then a voice came from heaven, "I have glorified it, and will glorify it again." [29] The crowd that was there and heard it said it had thundered; others said an angel had spoken to him.

30 Jesus said, "This voice was for your benefit, not mine. *31* Now is the time for judgment on this world; now the prince of this world will be driven out. *32* But I, when I am lifted up from the earth, will draw all men to myself." *33* He said this to show the kind of death he was going to die.

34 The crowd spoke up, "We have heard from the Law that the Christ will remain forever, so how can you say, 'The Son of Man must be lifted up'? Who is this 'Son of Man'?"

35 Then Jesus told them, "You are going to have the light just a little while longer. Walk while you have the light, before darkness overtakes you. The man who walks in the dark does not know where he is going. *36* Put your trust in the light while you have it, so that you may become sons of light." When he had finished speaking, Jesus left and hid himself from them.

QUESTIONS
FOR REVIEW

1. What stands out to you when you read this chapter?

   _____

   _____

   _____

2. Please comment on these scriptures:

   JOHN 1:29
   ²⁹The next day John saw Jesus coming toward him and said, "Look, the Lamb of God, who takes away the sin of the world!

   _____

   _____

   _____

   JOHN 1:36
   ³⁶When he saw Jesus passing by, he said, "Look, the Lamb of God!"

   _____

3. What is the most important thing that is restored to you through Jesus' death on the cross?

4. Please give your understanding about Jesus' statement that he is "the way and the truth and the life," (John 14:6).

QUESTIONS
FOR MEDITATION & APPLICATION

1. How do you evaluate the many kinds of wisdom in light of the fruits from the two trees?

2. The devil is the father of all lies. What kind of misconceptions did you have of the cross before reading this chapter?

3. We all know that Jesus died on the cross for the sins of the world. Is there anything more to the meaning and power of the cross beyond the forgiveness of our sins? Please explain.

_____

_____

4. Write something that "died" in you when you came to (or grew in) Christ.

_____

_____

_____

- Was it painful?

_____

_____

- Did you receive new life in an unexpected way?

_____

_____

5. Ask the Lord to show you what else needs to die in you. Please give an explanation of this.

_____

5

SONSHIP

OVERVIEW

In this chapter, we will visit the concept of sonship in God and its meaning and application to mankind:

- Sonship (birthright and inheritance)
- A review of sonship in the history of man
- Christ restored sonship to us
- Difference between a son and an orphan
- Going from adoption, to being about the Father's Business

SONSHIP IN THE GODHEAD

God's word (the expression of His thoughts and ways), many times, cannot not be understood via linear thinking which is confined by time. Time, in this context, is a power that works out life or death as it proceeds towards an end from a beginning. However, God's word exists in the eternal realm, and can be expressed in a sequential order to be actualized in our world as happenings, or events in time.

Our world, or as the early apostles called it, the cosmos, is the age of man with the current arrangement of the heavens and the earth. In the framework of human thought, the cosmos is most often understood from the perspective of a linear timeline. The reason for this is easy to discern: the human life experience, which is commonly confined by this world or within the earthly dimension, will always be regulated by the dimension of time. However, real spiritual life in God originates from the highest realm, the Eternal Realm, where He is. Even so, time will inevitably be influenced by and will influence the heavenly realms where God resides and moves, just like in the earthly realm. In the eternal realm, the end is the beginning, and is with the beginning. What is conceived in the eternal realm also conforms to the beginning, witnesses the beginning, and evolves or increases with the beginning, along with its nature and substance.

The Son and His Covenant with the Father

With this in mind, let us proceed to discuss the Beginning. God has never been confined in any form, visible or invisible. He expresses His love, power, wisdom, and perfection using all forms of creation or names (names that can be named). Yet He did not allow Himself to be found in any particular form until Christ was born. From the Beginning, God gave man the privilege to be an expression and a representation of Himself to the visible and the invisible world. However, His true desire for man was never just for man's wellbeing in this natural world. Rather, God created man to be a spiritual entity that would bear the fullness of His likeness (invisible). God would transform man from his lowly state into His own glorious being, even though man had been created in His image (visible). We have discussed this in previous chapters. Man was destined to share and to rule with God all that He created, visible and invisible, natural and spiritual. Man was to embody or to be the tabernacle (dwelling place) of God.

> **"God created man to be a spiritual entity that would bear the fullness of His likeness (invisible)."**

In essence, God the Father, before He created this world, had His sons, who are His heirs, in mind. His intention was that, through the race of mankind (a living being who is able to receive, apprehend, and represent His love and wisdom), He would be glorified with them in the sight of all creation. For unto man, He was pleased to impute the fullness of His nature and character. Through His love and fellowship with man, He would teach him all things. In summary, God the Father desires to create a race or family of sons, so that He can share his wisdom, love, and glory with them. This is the true essence of the gospel. Paul describes this very well:

> **EPHESIANS 1:4-6**
> *⁴ For he chose us in him before the creation of the world to be holy and blameless in his sight. In love ⁵ he predestined us to be adopted as his sons through Jesus Christ, in accordance with his pleasure and will—*
> *⁶ to the praise of his glorious grace, which he has freely given us in the One he loves.*

Now, in order to put in motion this "Word," or pattern life of the Son of God, God the Father did two things in the beginning:

First, He made an eternal covenant with His Son, the Christ, in whom He imputed all of Himself, even His very life and glory.

John would call the Son, the "Word of God." All things were created by Him, through Him, and for Him. In order to reveal His purpose and His love to His creation, God the Father set in motion a process to impart His honor and glory to the Son through His embodiment (indwelling) in man. His word has to be fulfilled through the instrumentality of the life of man. Man is to receive the glorification into God's very nature and being, as we discussed before. However, when the Son or

> **"God the Father desires to create a race or family of sons, so that He can share his wisdom, love, and glory with them."**

the Word (God's expressed will) was presented or revealed to the angelic realm, the devil rebelled against the wisdom of God in this choice. That is, to have man, a lower race in his sight, to receive the fullness of God's blessing, even His honor, glory, power, and life. Satan could not understand or embrace the plan that God, as a Father to His sons, would endow man with such a great love. So, he refused to bow and worship the Son with the Father, and rebelled against the eternal plan of God for man. That is why John in his first epistle says this:

1 JOHN 3:1-3
¹ See what great love the Father has lavished on us, that we should be called children of God! And that is what we are! The reason the world does not know us is that it did not know him. ² Dear friends, now we are children of God, and what we will be has not yet been made known. ³ But we know that when Christ appears, we shall be like him, for we shall see him as he is.

This is saying that the Christ, or the anointing that is to teach us all things about the Father and the Son, is now anointing us with spiritual understanding and wisdom. Thus, the Word of God becomes alive in us. This is what Jesus says in the gospel of John, that the Holy Spirit will reveal the Son and the Father to us, which will give us a new life in God. It is not merely talking about a future event, which will happen, but a progression that must be made by a son of God on his journey into spiritual maturity. Paul also spoke of this as his own experience:

GALATIANS 1:15-16
¹⁵ But when God, who set me apart from birth and called me by his grace, was pleased ¹⁶ to reveal his Son in me so that I might preach him among the Gentiles, I did not consult any man.

In the same epistle, John also shares that anyone who denies Jesus Christ came in the flesh is the antichrist. Why? Because such a denial is not merely about the particular historical happening concerning the coming of the Christ as Jesus the Nazarene. Rather, it has to do with God's original intent of having sons through those who choose to believe the Truth and live out His Word, even the very life of Christ Jesus, the Son of God. The perfection of man is that God Himself will dwell in his bodily form with His fullness, and He will transform or glorify the body of man from a natural one to a spiritual one, as Paul describes it:

COLOSSIANS 2:9-12
⁹ For in Christ all the fullness of the Deity lives in bodily form, ¹⁰ and you have been given fullness in Christ, who is the head over every power and authority. ¹¹ In him you were also circumcised, in the putting off of the sinful nature, not with a circumcision done by the hands of men but with the circumcision done by Christ, ¹² having been buried with him in baptism and raised with him through your faith in the power of God, who raised him from the dead.

PHILIPPIANS 3:20-21
²⁰ But our citizenship is in heaven. And we eagerly await a Savior from there, the Lord Jesus Christ, ²¹ who, by the power that enables him to bring everything under his control, will transform [is transforming] our lowly bodies so that they will be like his glorious body.

This should also be understood in the present tense as well. The power of resurrection is now imparting power and life to us through the in-dwelling of the Spirit of holiness.

1 CORINTHIANS 15:42-49

⁴² So will it be [is] with the resurrection of the dead. The body that is sown is perishable, it is raised imperishable; ⁴³ it is sown in dishonor, it is raised in glory; it is sown in weakness, it is raised in power; ⁴⁴ it is sown a natural body, it is raised a spiritual body. If there is a natural body, there is also a spiritual body. ⁴⁵ So it is written: "The first man Adam became a living being"; the last Adam, a life-giving spirit. ⁴⁶ The spiritual did not come first, but the natural, and after that the spiritual. ⁴⁷ The first man was of the dust of the earth, the second man from heaven. ⁴⁸ As was the earthly man, so are those who are of the earth; and as is the man from heaven, so also are those who are of heaven. ⁴⁹ And just as we have borne the likeness [image] of the earthly man, so shall we bear the likeness of the man from heaven.

In His sovereign knowledge and righteousness, God the Father allowed His decision to be challenged, so that His justice and power would prevail, and His wisdom and love would be fully revealed. His judgment and His goodness will then be proven unshakable.

Secondly, <u>He extended His eternal covenant to include man</u>, and with him, the whole creation. God's design was that man would have to exercise faith and love toward Him, and willingly subject himself to a process of being disciplined or discipled, in order to know Him and be like Him. He is God to all creation and Father to those who believe in His Son, the Word of God.

In essence, man was designed to become a template of a life of obedience by faith and of love unto God. The choice to believe and to joyfully obey God as Lord and Father is constantly before man.

Notice that the judgment of whether God is right or wrong was not absent when God created the visible world. Satan was given the opportunity to challenge and oppose, and man was given the freewill to trust and obey. This was represented by the existence of the tree of life and the tree of the knowledge of good and evil. God created the world or this age, placed man in the Garden of Eden, and then covenanted with Adam. Through this personal covenant, God's eternal covenant with His Son was then activated in mankind, via human flesh and soul, to embody the Spirit of sonship. He planted the seed of it in man (male and female) and granted them the full capacity to hear His voice, behold His face, learn His wisdom, and to receive and dispense His love. Also, because purity and holiness (being set apart) were endowed to him as a gift (birthright)—Man, in his natural being, would have the privilege to walk in the presence of God. All creation would witness this and thereby know God in His holiness, power, love, wisdom, righteousness, and goodness.

In summary, when God created man, He intended that man would have the fullness of His life given to him if he chose to listen and obey His Word, the promise or covenant of eternal life. That is why John mentioned in his gospel:

JOHN 1:1-4; 10-13
¹ In the beginning was the Word, and the Word was with God, and the Word was God. ² He was with God in the beginning. ³ Through him all things were made; without him nothing was made that has been made. ⁴ In him was life, and that life was the light of men...

¹⁰ He was in the world, and though the world was made through him, the world did not recognize him. ¹¹ He came to that which was his own, but his own did not receive him. ¹² Yet to all who received him, to those who believed in his name, he gave the right to become children of God— ¹³ children born not of a natural descent, nor of human decision or a husband's will, but born of God.

Paul commented on this often in the Book of Colossians.

COLOSSIANS 1:15-17
¹⁵ He [Christ] is the image of the invisible God, the firstborn over all creation. ¹⁶ For by him all things were created: things in heaven and on earth, visible and invisible, whether thrones or powers or rulers or authorities; all things were created by him and for him. ¹⁷ He is before all things, and in him all things hold together.

COLOSSIANS 1:27
²⁷ To them God has chosen to make known among the Gentiles the glorious riches of this mystery, which is Christ in you, the hope of glory.

Firstborn: Birthright and Inheritance

The concept of sonship clearly undergirds all of God's dealings with man throughout history. Let's examine the concept of the "firstborn," or "firstfruits," by taking a closer look at Colossians 1:15: "He [Christ Jesus] is the image of the invisible God", or as the author of Hebrews says, "the exact representation of His being."

We know that the invisible world includes angels and spiritual entities of various forms and ranks. There are a vast array of spiritual beings existing in the spiritual realm or world, and they were all created through Christ, by Him, and for Him. So was the whole universe created, or the visible world and everything in it. In other words, Christ precedes all created things.

This clearly implies the concept of firstborn. Christ is the firstborn of God's eternal life into creation. When man was separated from God, death entered the visible world, and man fell into the dominion of darkness. However, God by His grace, preserved man as a "spiritual womb," for the promised eternal life of God. Even so, this "womb" was not able to become one with, or produce, the spiritual seed for "that which is born of the flesh can only give birth to the flesh." In essence, the promise of God's spiritual life to mankind (man's divine birthright and promised inheritance) had become a desolate womb, incapable of giving or producing life in the Spirit of God. Man could however, still be touched or used by Him, as were the many godly men and prophets in the Old Testament. Even so, the promise of eternal life in God was not yet fulfilled.

This is why Jesus made a clear distinction in the book of Matthew between the fruits of his ministry and those of John the Baptist's, who was the greatest of all the prophets before him. Jesus said:

> **MATTHEW 11:10-11**
> *[10] This is the one (John the Baptist) about whom it is written:*
> *"'I will send my messenger ahead of you, who will prepare your way before you.'*
> *[11] I tell you the truth: Among those born of women there has not risen anyone greater than John the Baptist; yet he who is least in the*

kingdom of heaven is greater than he.

We are familiar with the fact that John was the one sent by God to give a testimony of Jesus as the Messiah (the Christ). However, the Messiah was more than a prophetic fulfillment of God's promised King and Savior to a particular people, namely the Jews. He was the one who would become Savior for all mankind, Jews and Gentiles alike. Through him, the promise and the power of God's eternal life is restored to all mankind. John was merely a messenger in the desolate land (the desert) of mankind, sent to make a proclamation of the coming of the Messiah. The seed of God's life was to be sown into the "promised land" of mankind, and to bring forth a great harvest of the sons of God. Jesus was the Seed or Branch that would bring forth a new linage of man—sons of God, not sons of Adam. That's why Paul would call believers "a new creation."

> **"The seed of God's life was to be sown into the 'promised land' of mankind, and to bring forth a great harvest of the sons of God."**

We can now see that man's hope for the eternal life of God was denied because of sin, which could only be taken away or redeemed by a perfect atonement. This atonement was required because of God's justice and the law of spiritual life in His holiness. The sinful nature or the flesh of man has to be abolished before he can partake in God's nature, so that he can be transformed into God's glory.

Now, what is the concept of "firstborn" in relationship to sonship in God?

God, the creator of all things, in His being, is self-sufficient. This means that He does not fit the mold of the roles and characters of man. He created and used them as types and shadows so that He can become the model (image) and the substance (likeness) that man desires and finds fulfillment in. So, in the Fatherhood of God, His being the Father is never to be understood as if He is a separate entity or person like our earthly father from our earthly mother. His Fatherhood is that He is the progenitor of His spiritual sons (descendants). This is especially true in His relationship to His only begotten Son. The Son is out of His being directly, which requires no vessel, nor a process of conception. The Son is the exact expression and embodiment of eternal life by the Spirit of the Father to mankind as the Model or Pattern Life (Dwelling Place, Form, Image)—as well as the Reality or Truth (Glory, Substance, Likeness). The Son becomes the image of His Father, not merely to the visible world, but also to the invisible spiritual realms. The Bible calls these the earth and the heavens.

In this light, sonship should be regarded as a positional and conceptual term, not one of gender. Sonship expresses itself in both genders in unity. That is why Paul mentions several times in his epistles that, "in Christ, there is no male or female." God the Father ordered the concept and ordinances of the "firstborn" within the family of man in order to make known His divine thoughts about His Son- "the mystery of Christ."

The firstborn son in the ancient Hebrew culture received two separate endowments from his father. One was his birthright, and the other was a double portion of the inheritance compared to that of his younger brothers.

This is clearly seen in the story of Jacob. First, he lured his twin brother, Esau, the natural firstborn, into exchanging his birthright for a bowl of soup. Then when Isaac was dying, Jacob pretended to be Esau at the encouragement of his mother, and stole their father's blessings for the firstborn from him. This can also be clearly seen in his own dealings with his sons when he passed on his blessings before his death. He gave Joseph a double portion and claimed Joseph's two sons, Manasseh and Ephraim, as his own. Interestingly, Ephraim, the second son of Joseph, thereby became the firstborn in the blessings of the family. This speaks of Jesus as the Covenant Restorer or Redeemer. The name Ephraim actually means "double portion" or "twice as fruitful." While Manasseh, the firstborn in the natural, means, "forget or being forgotten." This is speaking of Adam (the covenant violator and breaker) who was forgot or is being forgotten by his Father God and His Household. We know that Adam did indeed lose his inheritance, the homeland of Eden. In this divine drama, we see God the Father reversing the tragic fate of mankind as sons of Adam. They are redeemed through Jesus the Christ, "the last Adam," the True Man, His only begotten Son, and are restored to the rank of the Father's "firstborns." That is, restored back to the blessings of His eternal life and divine nature.

Now, here is another picture from ancient times. Having the birthright, the firstborn is destined to bear the name of the father. When the son has become mature, he is to represent his father in social and legal or covenantal matters. For this reason, he will be put into strict discipline by the father under the guidance of the household in the hands of the stewards (servants), who are familiar with the businesses of the family. In this way, he will be equipped with skills, knowledge, wisdom, and experiences to handle the responsibility of the family when he receives his inheritance. The name of the family goes with the birthright, and with it, honor and wellbeing. Furthermore, the firstborn is also entrusted with the duty to watch over his siblings and to help them manage their affairs, so that they all can live together in wisdom, unity, love and prosperity as one family.

In this, we can clearly see the underlying revelation of the author of Hebrews and why he said that, "the Christ is the firstborn among many brothers." Paul called him the "firstfruits among many." He is not ashamed to call his disciples brothers and friends, because truly they were made so by the love of the Father, their faith in the Son, and by His finished work on their behalf. The Son chose to more than empty himself of his heavenly blessings and privileges, lay down his honor and royalty to wash our feet as a humble servant, but he also willingly laid down his life for us on the cross so that we could be reconciled back to the Father. Is there any love greater than this? Bless His Holy Name! This is the gospel and the Truth He gives to us. Freely!

With the inheritance, the firstborn receives the privilege of a double-portion. This double-portion, however, was passed on to the Church, or the called-out ones in Christ Jesus (see Isaiah 61). Our double portion is the Father and the Son. Our inheritance is God Himself, and we are also His inheritance.

SONSHIP IN THE HISTORY OF MAN

Now, in this light, let's review the concept of sonship throughout the history of mankind.

Adam and Eve

God created Adam and Eve to be one. As mentioned above, in sonship, there is no male nor female. In this "oneness" is the hidden mystery of the Christ and his Bride, the Church. He is the Head of the Church and they are one Body. Actually, before the Fall, it was Adam who called woman, "woman." In Hebrew, it sounds the same as man, which implies Adam named her after his own name. In terms of oneness, they are indeed on equal ground in the eyes of God concerning His covenant with man.

This oneness has numerous facets. Here are a few:

1. Oneness of flesh and blood in their communion of human intimacy and cooperation as natural beings

2. Oneness of mind and soul in their communion of human conscience and understanding as conscious beings

3. Oneness of heart and spirit in their communion of spiritual intimacy and agreement as spiritual beings

4. Oneness of love and wisdom in the counsel and power of God the Father, who is the Spirit

5. Oneness of destiny in God. In this blessing of oneness

with God and with each other, they were destined to mature in wisdom and love, and eventually their natural beings would be fully transformed into the life or being of God, His very nature and glory. They were to learn to manage things on His behalf, and eventually to rule with Him in His Kingdom.

However, after the Fall, God's judgment made it impossible for Adam to treat Eve as an equal partner (helper) anymore. Man was put in a place to rule over woman, because it was through woman that man was deceived. So, Adam changed the name of woman to "Eve," which means "living," because she would become the mother of all the living. Interestingly, when they had children, Eve was the one to name them. So, in essence, none were named by Adam (man), rather they were named by Eve (woman). You know the story, God also put enmity between her seed and the seed of the serpent. Man lost the blessings of the name of God and had to suffer the wound and pain of the poisoning of his mind by a false wisdom or darkened counsel which had come from the Deceiver, the devil.

As the apostle John clearly points out, the core of the devil's deception was to deny man, a being in the flesh, his birthright and inheritance as a son of God.

JOHN 4:1-3
¹ Dear friends, do not believe every spirit, but test the spirits to see whether they are from God, because many false prophets have gone out into the world. ² This is how you can recognize the Spirit of God: Every spirit that acknowledges that Jesus Christ has come in the flesh (in the lives of Jesus and His believers) is from God, ³ but

every spirit that does not acknowledge Jesus is not from God. This is the spirit of the antichrist, which you have heard is coming and even now is already in the world.

In the covenant with God, a covenant of peace and life, Adam was equally yoked with the woman, yet he is the one whom God held accountable for its fulfillment. Unfortunately, when Eve sinned, he did not intervene in the process. Instead, he ended up being a participant in her rebellion. Sadly, this imprudent act broke their oneness and produced a separation between them in God's sight, so they were judged separately. And through this judgment, eternal life was separated from man, and thus ended the blessedness of a oneness that God intended for them, with Him, and with each other. The womb of mankind was denied the planting or seeding of the Spirit of sonship. Man was separated from God and denied the benefit of the eternal covenant.

The Seed of Promise

God never broke His covenant with His Son. However, throughout the ages He preserved a seed to carry the hope and promise of His life in the natural lineage of mankind. This was so that in the fullness of time, He would take away the sinful nature from man, and plant the seed of the Spirit of sonship in him yet gain.

After righteous Abel was killed, death entered the family of man. In Abel's place, God gave Adam and Eve another son, whose name was Seth. Now Seth was named by Eve, but he was in Adam's image and likeness, which was a token of a kind of restoration for the things of God in the family of man.

From the line of Seth, the bloodshed of killing one's brother was not counted, although his decedents did inherit the fallen nature of man, meaning that they were not immune to sin. Still, in His rich mercy and faithfulness, God preserved through them "a seed," with the promise of His life for mankind. This went on until the time of Noah. Judgment came upon the earth and only Noah and his family were saved. One of his sons, Shem, was reserved as the firstborn to inherit the covenant God had made with his father Noah until the time of Abram.

> **"In His rich mercy and faithfulness, God preserved through them 'a seed,' with the promise of His life for mankind."**

God called Abram to move with his family out from the Chaldeans. In the process, they stopped at Haran. Then God called Abram to move on to the land He promised that He would give to his descendants. During this journey of faith, God made a covenant with Abram (exalted father) and changed his name to Abraham (father of many). As He promised, He also gave him a son, Isaac, who was a type of Christ. (There is much that can be expounded about the story of Abraham and his wives and two sons, Ishmael and Isaac. Paul comments on this in Galatians 4.)

From Jacob, David, and Solomon, to the restoration after the Babylonian Exile, the story of the Israelites is quite familiar to us, so we will not get into those details here.

CHRIST RESTORED SONSHIP TO US

God allowed the Israelites to be enslaved in Egypt for over 400 years until He raised up Moses to deliver them. On Mount Sinai, He gave them the law through Moses and His angels. In the law, the particulars about the firstborn and the father-son relationship are very illuminating.

> **DEUTERONOMY 21:15–23**
> *[15] If a man has two wives, and he loves one but not the other, and both bear him sons but the firstborn is the son of the wife he does not love, [16] when he wills his property to his sons, he must not give the rights of the firstborn to the son of the wife he loves in preference to his actual firstborn, the son of the wife he does not love. [17] He must acknowledge the son of his unloved wife as the firstborn by giving him a double share of all he has. That son is the first sign of his father's strength. The right of the firstborn belongs to him.*
>
> *[18] If a man has a stubborn and rebellious son who does not obey his father and mother and will not listen to them when they discipline him, [19] his father and mother shall take hold of him and bring him to the elders at the gate of his town. [20] They shall say to the elders, "This son of ours is stubborn and rebellious. He will not obey us. He is a profligate and a drunkard." [21] Then all the men of his town shall stone him to death. You must purge the evil from among you. All Israel will hear of it and be afraid.*
>
> *[22] If a man guilty of a capital offense is put to death and his body is hung on a tree, [23] you must not leave his body on the tree overnight. Be sure to bury him that same day, because anyone who is hung on a tree is under God's curse. You must not desecrate the land the Lord*

your God is giving you as an inheritance.

In the law, God ordained the right of the firstborn and the death penalty of a rebellious son. Notice, one who is punished with death as a rebellious son is to be hung on a tree. He should not be left there overnight, or it will desecrate the land as the inheritance. Every detail here is speaking of certain aspects of Christ's death on the cross. Jesus Christ took away the curse that, through Adam, was upon man, and restored man's rights as the firstborn back to him, as well as his previously lost inheritance in God the Father. Our Lord Jesus Christ, as the last Adam, stepped into the place of the first Adam. Eve had been barren in the sense that she was not able to produce sons of God, as was her original destiny as the "mother of the living." Now in a spiritual and symbolic way, Jesus opened this "womb" as the last Adam, making the way for many sons of God to be produced.

This fulfilled the prophecy given by Isaiah. Mentioned here are a number of them, as well as Paul's comments, to show the importance of this.

ISAIAH 49:8–26
⁸ This is what the Lord says:
"In the time of my favor I will answer you, and in the day of salvation I will help you; I will keep you and will make you to be a covenant for the people, to restore the land and to reassign its desolate inheritances,
⁹ to say to the captives, 'Come out,' and to those in darkness, 'Be free!' "They will feed beside the roads and find pasture on every barren hill.
¹⁰ They will neither hunger nor thirst, nor will the desert heat or the

sun beat down on them. He who has compassion on them will guide them and lead them beside springs of water.
[11] I will turn all my mountains into roads, and my highways will be raised up.
[12] See, they will come from afar—some from the north, some from the west, some from the region of Aswan."
[13] Shout for joy, you heavens; rejoice, you earth; burst into song, you mountains! For the Lord comforts his people and will have compassion on his afflicted ones.
[14] But Zion said, "The Lord has forsaken me, the Lord has forgotten me."
[15] "Can a mother forget the baby at her breast and have no compassion on the child she has borne? Though she may forget, I will not forget you!
[16] See, I have engraved you on the palms of my hands; your walls are ever before me.
[17] Your children hasten back, and those who laid you waste depart from you.
[18] Lift up your eyes and look around; all your children gather and come to you. As surely as I live," declares the Lord, "you will wear them all as ornaments; you will put them on, like a bride.
[19] "Though you were ruined and made desolate and your land laid waste, now you will be too small for your people, and those who devoured you will be far away.
[20] The children born during your bereavement will yet say in your hearing, 'This place is too small for us; give us more space to live in.'
[21] Then you will say in your heart, 'Who bore me these? I was bereaved and barren; I was exiled and rejected. Who brought these up? I was left all alone, but these—where have they come from?'"
[22] This is what the Sovereign Lord says: "See, I will beckon to the nations, I will lift up my banner to the peoples; they will bring your

sons in their arms and carry your daughters on their hips.
²³ Kings will be your foster fathers, and their queens your nursing mothers. They will bow down before you with their faces to the ground; they will lick the dust at your feet. Then you will know that I am the Lord; those who hope in me will not be disappointed."
²⁴ Can plunder be taken from warriors, or captives be rescued from the fierce?
²⁵ But this is what the Lord says: "Yes, captives will be taken from warriors, and plunder retrieved from the fierce; I will contend with those who contend with you, and your children I will save.
²⁶ I will make your oppressors eat their own flesh; they will be drunk on their own blood, as with wine. Then all mankind will know that I, the Lord, am your Savior, your Redeemer, the Mighty One of Jacob."

ISAIAH 54:1–13

¹ "Sing, barren woman, you who never bore a child; burst into song, shout for joy, you who were never in labor; because more are the children of the desolate woman than of her who has a husband," says the Lord.
² "Enlarge the place of your tent, stretch your tent curtains wide, do not hold back; lengthen your cords, strengthen your stakes.
³ For you will spread out to the right and to the left; your descendants will dispossess nations and settle in their desolate cities.
⁴ " Do not be afraid; you will not be put to shame. Do not fear disgrace; you will not be humiliated. You will forget the shame of your youth and remember no more the reproach of your widowhood.
⁵ For your Maker is your husband—the Lord Almighty is his name—the Holy One of Israel is your Redeemer; he is called the God of all the earth.
⁶ The Lord will call you back as if you were a wife deserted and distressed in spirit—a wife who married young, only to be rejected,"

THE SEED

says your God.
⁷ "For a brief moment I abandoned you, but with deep compassion I will bring you back.
⁸ In a surge of anger I hid my face from you for a moment, but with everlasting kindness I will have compassion on you," says the Lord your Redeemer.
⁹ "To me this is like the days of Noah, when I swore that the waters of Noah would never again cover the earth. So now I have sworn not to be angry with you, never to rebuke you again.
¹⁰ Though the mountains be shaken and the hills be removed, yet my unfailing love for you will not be shaken nor my covenant of peace be removed," says the Lord, who has compassion on you.
¹¹ "Afflicted city, lashed by storms and not comforted, I will rebuild you with stones of turquoise, your foundations with lapis lazuli.
¹² I will make your battlements of rubies, your gates of sparkling jewels, and all your walls of precious stones.
¹³ All your children will be taught by the Lord, and great will be their peace.

ISAIAH 62:1-5
¹ For Zion's sake I will not keep silent, for Jerusalem's sake I will not remain quiet, till her vindication shines out like the dawn, her salvation like a blazing torch.
² The nations will see your vindication, and all kings your glory; you will be called by a new name that the mouth of the Lord will bestow.
³ You will be a crown of splendor in the Lord's hand, a royal diadem in the hand of your God.
⁴ No longer will they call you Deserted, or name your land Desolate. But you will be called Hephzibah, and your land Beulah; for the Lord will take delight in you, and your land will be married.
⁵ As a young man marries a young woman, so will your Builder

[sons] marry you; as a bridegroom rejoices over his bride, so will your God rejoice over you.

GALATIANS 4:26–31
²⁶ But the Jerusalem that is above is free, and she is our mother. ²⁷ For it is written:
"Be glad, barren woman, you who never bore a child; shout for joy and cry aloud, you who were never in labor; because more are the children of the desolate woman than of her who has a husband."
²⁸ Now you, brothers and sisters, like Isaac, are children of promise. ²⁹ At that time the son born according to the flesh persecuted the son born by the power of the Spirit. It is the same now. ³⁰ But what does Scripture say? "Get rid of the slave woman and her son, for the slave woman's son will never share in the inheritance with the free woman's son." ³¹ Therefore, brothers and sisters, we are not children of the slave woman, but of the free woman.

There is actually another ancient ordinance in the family of the people of God. It was customary for a brother to marry the widow of his elder brother. Their firstborn son would be then named after his elder brother and thus entitled as the rightful heir for his brother. This was to preserve the name or linage of his brother. This also speaks of the redemptive nature of Jesus' life and ministry. He became the firstborn among the living, and is therefore able to grant eternal life to others. This is a well-established theme throughout the Bible. Let's just look at a few passages:

COLOSSIANS 1:18–20
¹⁸ And he is the head of the body, the church; he is the beginning and the firstborn from among the dead, so that in everything he might

have the supremacy. *¹⁹ For God was pleased to have all his fullness dwell in him, ²⁰ and through him to reconcile to himself all things, whether things on earth or things in heaven, by making peace through his blood, shed on the cross.*

1 CORINTHIANS 15:20–22

²⁰ But Christ has indeed been raised from the dead, the firstfruits of those who have fallen asleep. ²¹ For since death came through a man, the resurrection of the dead comes also through a man. ²² For as in Adam all die, so in Christ all will be made alive.

PSALM 89:19–29

*¹⁹ Once you spoke in a vision,
to your faithful people you said:
"I have bestowed strength on a warrior;
I have exalted a young man from among the people.
²⁰ I have found David my servant;
with my sacred oil I have anointed him.
²¹ My hand will sustain him;
surely my arm will strengthen him.
²² No enemy will subject him to tribute;
no wicked man will oppress him.
²³ I will crush his foes before him
and strike down his adversaries.
²⁴ My faithful love will be with him,
and through my name his horn will be exalted.
²⁵ I will set his hand over the sea,
his right hand over the rivers.
²⁶ He will call out to me, 'You are my Father,
my God, the Rock my Savior.'
²⁷ I will also appoint him my firstborn,
the most exalted of the kings of the earth.*

²⁸ I will maintain my love to him forever,
and my covenant with him will never fail.
²⁹ I will establish his line forever,
*his throne as long as the heavens endure.*ᶜ

HEBREWS 2:9-11
⁹ But we see Jesus, who was made a little lower than the angels, now crowned with glory and honor because he suffered death, so that by the grace of God he might taste death for everyone.
¹⁰ In bringing many sons to glory, it was fitting that God, for whom and through whom everything exists, should make the author of their salvation perfect through suffering. ¹¹ Both the one who makes men holy and those who are made holy are of the same family. So Jesus is not ashamed to call them brothers.

He did this by sending His Holy Spirit, the Spirit of sonship, the promised gift from God the Father.

Most of us are quite familiar with the concept of being "born-again." It has become a buzz word for becoming a Christian. But to be born again is not just a change of faith in the context of any religious practice or encampment. It is a spiritual reality and an experience that one must possess in order to be saved, and to live the life of the Spirit. Only by this will we know how to live as a son of God. When we received the seed of the Spirit of sonship, just like Jesus was born of the Holy Spirit, we are sealed for a work of transformation. It takes a period of time for the maturing of our spirit, not to mention our soul

---

ᶜ This is a messianic Psalm. The references about David are actually speaking about Jesus Christ.

and flesh, for us to be fully immersed into this reality and live in its ways or laws. Paul describes it well:

> **ROMANS 8:13-17**
> *¹³ For if you live according to the sinful nature, you will die; but if by the Spirit you put to death the misdeeds of the body, you will live. ¹⁴ because those who are led by the Spirit of God are sons of God. ¹⁵ For you did not receive a spirit that makes you a slave again to fear, but you received the Spirit of sonship. And by him we cry, "Abba, Father." ¹⁶ The Spirit himself testifies with our spirit that we are God's children. ¹⁷ Now if we are children, then we are heirs—heirs of God and co-heirs with Christ, if indeed we share in his sufferings in order that we may also share in his glory.*

Remember, in this, there is neither male nor female. It is like an orphan is adopted by a new family and is embraced gradually by the love of the father and mother. We go from being a total stranger to being an integral member of the family. We become acquainted with the ways of the family, the love of the parents, and the privilege of the family name, culture, and inheritance.

The example of adoption can only reflect certain aspects of this process. But there is something more to our own wellbeing as a man that used to be alienated from the love of God, something miraculous in nature and power. It is the new life of a blessed son, not an orphan. The orphaned soul is forever wandering and searching for a family where he will receive love and a sense of belonging.

SON AND ORPHAN

It is evident that when Adam was judged by God as unfit for His life, a life without sin and full of goodness, he was discarded from God's Household as a son. In this is the essence of the story of the prodigal son, who lost his privileges in his father's family and went on in his own way. Sin has made us all orphans to God as sons of Adam. But through Christ Jesus and our faith in him, we are restored to God the Father and His Household. Much could be said if we were to expound on this. One thing, however, that is always worth emphasizing, is that God the Father never wants anyone to live as an orphan. Though they might have to go through terrible things in life as the result of a corrupted world, laden with the sins of men and the deceptions of the evil one, the Father always wants us to come back to His home as His beloved sons.

PSALM 68:5-6
⁵ A father to the fatherless, a defender of widows,
is God in his holy dwelling.
⁶ God sets the lonely in families,
he leads forth the prisoners with singing;
but the rebellious live in a sun-scorched land.

This is the very core and essence of the teachings of Jesus, the Word of God. That is that through our faith in him, we will be restored back to the Father.

JOHN 14:1-18
¹ "Do not let your hearts be troubled. You believe in God; believe also in me. ² My Father's house has many rooms; if that were not so,

would I have told you that I am going there to prepare a place for you? ³ And if I go and prepare a place for you, I will come back and take you to be with me that you also may be where I am. ⁴ You know the way to the place where I am going."
⁵ Thomas said to him, "Lord, we don't know where you are going, so how can we know the way?"
⁶ Jesus answered, "I am the way and the truth and the life. No one comes to the Father except through me. ⁷ If you really know me, you will known my Father as well. From now on, you do know him and have seen him."
⁸ Philip said, "Lord, show us the Father and that will be enough for us."
⁹ Jesus answered: "Don't you know me, Philip, even after I have been among you such a long time? Anyone who has seen me has seen the Father. How can you say, 'Show us the Father'? ¹⁰ Don't you believe that I am in the Father, and that the Father is in me? The words I say to you I do not speak on my own authority. Rather, it is the Father, living in me, who is doing his work. ¹¹ Believe me when I say that I am in the Father and the Father is in me; or at least believe on the evidence of the works themselves. ¹² Very truly I tell you, whoever believes in me will do the works I have been doing, and they will do even greater things than these, because I am going to the Father. ¹³ And I will do whatever you ask in my name, so that the Father may be glorified in the Son. ¹⁴ You may ask me for anything in my name, and I will do it.

¹⁵ "If you love me, keep my commands. ¹⁶ And I will ask the Father, and he will give you another advocate to help you and be with you forever— ¹⁷ the Spirit of truth. The world cannot accept him, because it neither sees him nor knows him. But you know him, for he lives with you and will be in you. ¹⁸ I will not leave you as orphans; I will come to you.

JOHN 15:15-16

[15] *I no longer call you servants, because a servant does not know his master's business. Instead, I have called you friends, for everything that I learned from my Father I have made known to you.* *[16]* *You did not choose me, but I chose you and appointed you to go and bear fruit—fruit that will last. Then the Father will give you whatever you ask in my name.*

JOHN 16:23-28

[23] *In that day you will no longer ask me anything. I tell you the truth, my Father will give you whatever you ask in my name.* *[24]* *Until now you have not asked for anything in my name. Ask and you will receive, and your joy will be complete.*
[25] *"Though I have been speaking figuratively, a time is coming when I will no longer use this kind of language but will tell you plainly about my Father.* *[26]* *In that day you will ask in my name. I am not saying that I will ask the Father on your behalf.* *[27]* *No, the Father himself loves you because you have loved me and have believed that I came from God.* *[28]* *I came from the Father and entered the world; now I am leaving the world and going back to the Father."*

JOHN 17:13-26

[13] *"I am coming to you now, but I say these things while I am still in the world, so that they may have the full measure of my joy within them.* *[14]* *I have given them your word and the world has hated them, for they are not of the world any more than I am of the world.* *[15]* *My prayer is not that you take them out of the world but that you protect them from the evil one.* *[16]* *They are not of the world, even as I am not of it.* *[17]* *Sanctify them by the truth; your word is truth.* *[18]* *As you sent me into the world, I have sent them into the world.* *[19]* *For them I sanctify myself, that they too may be truly sanctified.*

The Seed

[20] "My prayer is not for them alone. I pray also for those who will believe in me through their message, [21] that all of them may be one, Father, just as you are in me and I am in you. May they also be in us so that the world may believe that you have sent me. [22] I have given them the glory that you gave me, that they may be one as we are one: [23] I in them and you in me. May they be brought to complete unity to let the world know that you sent me and have loved them even as you have loved me.

[24] "Father, I want those you have given me to be with me where I am, and to see my glory, the glory you have given me because you loved me before the creation of the world.

[25] "Righteous Father, though the world does not know you, I know you, and they know that you have sent me. [26] I have made you known to them, and will continue to make you known in order that the love you have for me may be in them and that I myself may be in them."

JOHN 20:16-18

[16] Jesus said to her, "Mary."
She turned toward him and cried out in Aramaic, "Rabboni!" (which means Teacher).
[17] Jesus said, "Do not hold on to me, for I have not yet returned to the Father. Go instead to my brothers and tell them, 'I am returning to my Father and your Father, to my God and your God.'"
[18] Mary Magdalene went to the disciples with the news: "I have seen the Lord!" And she told them that he had said these things to her.

Now we can see that through his teachings, Jesus was able to make the Father known to the disciples and had them firmly planted in the hope and faith extending from His word, even the promise of eternal life in God as sons of God. He had also equipped them with wisdom and power to go about preaching and teaching this message, which is the Gospel of the Kingdom. The mission was to free others from their sins and the corrupt world, so they too could be reconciled to the Father Himself as sons of God. I think it would be helpful for us to take a brief look in a general sense at some of the differences between an orphan and a son.

1. Family Love: A son is free to receive love from members of the family and free to offer his love and affection to others. An orphan is often fearful to do so.

2. Inheritance: A son has the right to claim his father's inheritance. An orphan has nothing to inherit. As a result, an orphan often carries with him either a sense of failure, or a pride of being "self-made." Either way, he is more likely to be burdened with the worries and anxieties of life. A son, on the other hand, enjoys the natural posture of being assured of everything, especially his future.

3. Provision and Protection: A son freely enjoys his father's protection and provision. These are absent for an orphan for the lack of a father. An orphan often struggles with the feeling of insecurity and falls prey to a spirit of fear and lack.

4. Mental and Emotional Wellbeing: A son, with a good up-bringing and healthy education, is likely to be stable in his mental and emotional expressions of himself. He enjoys great security, stability, and confidence because of who he is. An orphan, lacking these, seldom is wholesome in his thinking and emotions and thus often appears to be

unstable in his expression of himself, being it mentally or emotionally—not to mention spiritually.

When Jesus was with his disciples, he shared with them that he would lead them to the Father—his Father and their Father. When he was ready to die, he encouraged them with the thought that he would not leave them as orphans.

By the Adamic nature, we have all lost the spiritual sense of being at home in life and love. We were all cast out, spiritually, from the presence of our heavenly Father. Only when we receive the Spirit of sonship are we able to be restored to our relationship with our heavenly Father, and that takes a process. It cannot be done by self-will and self-strength, but only by the apprehension and appropriation of His grace and love through Christ Jesus.

FROM ADOPTION, TO BEING "ABOUT THE FATHER'S BUSINESS"

First, we are adopted back into the Family of God and begin to fellowship with Him as a son would with his father. Second, we will live in His love, security, and provision. Even more than that, the Father will begin to teach us about Himself and impart His own likeness to us. The Father's heart is to have mature sons, not just infants and toddlers. This takes a process. Let's look at what Peter said about this.

> **2 PETER 1:3–8**
> *³ His divine power has given us everything we need for life and godliness through our knowledge of him who called us by his own*

glory and goodness. ⁴ Through these he has given us his very great and precious promises, so that through them you may participate in the divine nature and escape the corruption in the world caused by evil desires.

⁵ For this very reason, make every effort to add to your faith goodness; and to goodness, knowledge; ⁶ and to knowledge, self-control; and to self-control, perseverance; and to perseverance, godliness; ⁷ and to godliness, brotherly kindness; and to brotherly kindness, love. ⁸ For if you possess these qualities in increasing measure, they will keep you from being ineffective and unproductive in your knowledge of our Lord Jesus Christ.

Then, how do we come to maturity?

1. We must have faith and hope in Jesus Christ.

2. We will have to learn obedience to God the Father through discipline.

This is the journey of our spiritual life in time and space. Jesus learned obedience from the things he suffered, and so will we. If we are to be like him, we must yield to the Father's discipline and partake of His divine nature in the life of His Son. This is love, righteousness, wisdom, peace, joy, power, mercy and goodness. The Father's desire is to have us mature in Him and become worthy of His name, so that we can reveal and teach all creation His love, wisdom, and justice. Are you ready for this journey?

SCRIPTURES

The "History" of Sonship

MATTHEW 22:41–46

[41] *While the Pharisees were gathered together, Jesus asked them,* [42] *"What do you think about the Christ? Whose son is he?"*
"The son of David," they replied.
[43] *He said to them, "How is it then that David, speaking by the Spirit, calls him 'Lord'? For he says,*
[44] *" 'The Lord said to my Lord: "Sit at my right hand until I put your enemies under your feet." '*
[45] *If then David calls him 'Lord,' how can he be his son?"* [46] *No one could say a word in reply, and from that day on no one dared to ask him any more questions.*

LUKE 15:11–32

[11] *Jesus continued: "There was a man who had two sons.* [12] *The younger one said to his father, 'Father, give me my share of the estate.' So he divided his property between them.*
[13] *"Not long after that, the younger son got together all he had, set off for a distant country and there squandered his wealth in wild living.*
[14] *After he had spent everything, there was a severe famine in that whole country, and he began to be in need.* [15] *So he went and hired himself out to a citizen of that country, who sent him to his fields to feed pigs.* [16] *He longed to fill his stomach with the pods that the pigs were eating, but no one gave him anything.*
[17] *"When he came to his senses, he said, 'How many of my father's hired men have food to spare, and here I am starving to death!* [18] *I will set out and go back to my father and say to him: Father, I have sinned against heaven and against you.* [19] *I am no longer worthy to be called*

your son; make me like one of your hired men.' ²⁰ *So he got up and went to his father.*

"*But while he was still a long way off, his father saw him and was filled with compassion for him; he ran to his son, threw his arms around him and kissed him.*
²¹ "*The son said to him, 'Father, I have sinned against heaven and against you. I am no longer worthy to be called your son.'*
²² "*But the father said to his servants, 'Quick! Bring the best robe and put it on him. Put a ring on his finger and sandals on his feet. ²³ Bring the fattened calf and kill it. Let's have a feast and celebrate. ²⁴ For this son of mine was dead and is alive again; he was lost and is found.' So they began to celebrate.*
²⁵ "*Meanwhile, the older son was in the field. When he came near the house, he heard music and dancing. ²⁶ So he called one of the servants and asked him what was going on. ²⁷ 'Your brother has come,' he replied, 'and your father has killed the fattened calf because he has him back safe and sound.'*
²⁸ "*The older brother became angry and refused to go in. So his father went out and pleaded with him. ²⁹ But he answered his father, 'Look! All these years I've been slaving for you and never disobeyed your orders. Yet you never gave me even a young goat so I could celebrate with my friends. ³⁰ But when this son of yours who has squandered your property with prostitutes comes home, you kill the fattened calf for him!'*
³¹ "'*My son,' the father said, 'you are always with me, and everything I have is yours. ³² But we had to celebrate and be glad, because this brother of yours was dead and is alive again; he was lost and is found.'"*

GALATIANS 4:4–7

⁴ *But when the time had fully come, God sent his Son, born of a woman, born under law, ⁵ to redeem those under law, that we might receive the full rights of sons. ⁶ Because you are sons, God sent the Spirit of his Son into our hearts, the Spirit who calls out, "Abba, Father." ⁷ So you are no longer*

a slave, but a son; and since you are a son, God has made you also an heir.

Son and Orphan

JOHN 14:15–19

¹⁵ "If you love me, you will obey what I command. ¹⁶ And I will ask the Father, and he will give you another Counselor to be with you forever— ¹⁷ the Spirit of truth. The world cannot accept him, because it neither sees him nor knows him. But you know him, for he lives with you and will be in you. ¹⁸ I will not leave you as orphans; I will come to you. ¹⁹ Before long, the world will not see me anymore, but you will see me. Because I live, you also will live.

MATTHEW 5:43–48

⁴³ "You have heard that it was said, 'Love your neighbor and hate your enemy.' ⁴⁴ But I tell you: Love your enemies and pray for those who persecute you, ⁴⁵ that you may be sons of your Father in heaven. He causes his sun to rise on the evil and the good, and sends rain on the righteous and the unrighteous. ⁴⁶ If you love those who love you, what reward will you get? Are not even the tax collectors doing that? ⁴⁷ And if you greet only your brothers, what are you doing more than others? Do not even pagans do that? ⁴⁸ Be perfect, therefore, as your heavenly Father is perfect.

HEBREWS 12:4–11

⁴ In your struggle against sin, you have not yet resisted to the point of shedding your blood. ⁵ And you have forgotten that word of encouragement that addresses you as sons:

"My son, do not make light of the Lord's discipline, and do not lose heart when he rebukes you, ⁶ because the Lord disciplines those he loves, and he punishes everyone he accepts as a son."

⁷ Endure hardship as discipline; God is treating you as sons. For what son is not disciplined by his father? ⁸ If you are not disciplined (and everyone undergoes discipline), then you are illegitimate children and not true sons. ⁹ Moreover, we have all had human fathers who disciplined us and we respected them for it. How much more should we submit to the Father of our spirits and live! ¹⁰ Our fathers disciplined us for a little while as they thought best; but God disciplines us for our good, that we may share in his holiness. ¹¹ No discipline seems pleasant at the time, but painful. Later on, however, it produces a harvest of righteousness and peace for those who have been trained by it.

QUESTIONS FOR REVIEW

1. We now know that our sonship in God through Christ Jesus is not based on gender. How does this revelation change the way you see yourself as a spiritual man in God?

_____

_____

_____

2. What are the major differences between the following relationships: a man who worships God and a man who is a spiritual son of God?

_____

_____

_____

3. Please offer your thoughts on the concept of the Fatherhood of God.

_____

4. Please revisit the story of Esau and Jacob in light of our spiritual birthright and inheritance as a son of God. Why do you think God would "hate" Esau and "love" Jacob (Malachi 1:1–5)?

QUESTIONS
FOR MEDITATION & APPLICATION

1. How do you exercise your living "faith" as a son of God according to the Gospel of the Kingdom of God? What is the difference between the "hope" and "faith" we have in Christ Jesus, in comparison with what is often presented to us by others in modern Christianity?

_____

_____

_____

2. Consider the differences between a spiritual "orphan" and a spiritual "son." How would they apply to mankind in general?

_____

_____

_____

3. How would they apply to you?

_____

4. In the light of your sonship in God, write down some thoughts about the true nature of discipleship in Jesus Christ.

6

SPIRITUAL LIFE

OVERVIEW

In this chapter, we will survey life in the Holy Spirit:

- Natural Life

- Spiritual Life

- Spiritual Food

- Spiritual Growth and Maturity

In the previous chapters, we mentioned that God created everything through Christ, His Son, both visible and invisible. When Adam sinned, man was "cast out" of the invisible, spiritual world into the visible, physical world and was bound by it. We will refer to this as the life of the "natural man." However, when one is born again through faith in Christ Jesus, and the receiving of the Spirit of sonship, he begins to have a life with access to God's presence and His spiritual reality. We will refer to this as the life of our "spiritual man."

God is good at using natural things to teach us spiritual realities. For a child of God, most understanding and wisdom is learned through the natural first, and then the spiritual. In this light, it is helpful to consider how we grow in natural stature and wisdom in order to gain insight of the spiritual life into which we are destined to mature.

THE LIFE OF THE NATURAL MAN

When life begins in a mother's womb via conception, it starts as a seed (neither male nor female). In a normal pregnancy, there is a set period of time for the body and its organs to form in the womb and become a healthy baby. When the child comes out of the womb, it will instantly begin to face a new world. Within the first few moments outside the womb, all the organs and other faculties of life will be quickened and utilized to adapt to the new environment. This is more than just entering into a new reality; it is a transforming experience, and is miraculous in many ways.

The Seed

Envision the life of a plant, like a tree. It takes a long time for the life within the seed to be released. It has to break out of the shell and take root. Gentle and fragile as it is in the beginning, it starts to take off on a journey of new life, no longer as a seed, but as a plant. Even so, it still takes a long time for it to grow strong enough to come out of the ground, and embrace the world of sunlight and wind. God so perfectly orders the seasons that this amazing process almost slips out of the scrutiny of our naked eyes, without our notice and appreciation. Yet each step in coming into a new world and in being strengthened as a new life is truly a miracle and a triumph for a life of such a humble beginning.

Similarly, a new-born baby is such a miracle and a triumph of life. The transformation and release is a wonder that combines both the breaking through the shell, like the tiny seed, as well as the coming out of the ground like a gentle shoot. Let's make some brief observations of this process in the life of a baby:

1. It initiates the opening of the natural senses, which will be fully utilized in a world full of wonders and new possibilities.

2. It begins to develop into a life of intelligence with knowledge, understanding, and wisdom.

3. The method of physical provision is totally changed. The baby no longer depends on the mother for nourishment. It begins to be fed or feed itself by mouth, first with milk, then as it grows, with solid food.

4. It is no longer isolated. As its emotional and mental

capacities are developed, the child will enjoy diverse relationships with others, first within the family, and then into a community and society, or culture.

Now, as the child grows in physical and mental stature, he will eventually grow into a mature man, having the full capacity and ability to cope with the natural world and find himself at home in it. He will also learn and create, using his knowledge, skills, and talents to fulfill tasks and responsibilities of all kinds. Most importantly, he will know how to receive and express love in a way that he had no clue about when he was in his mother's womb.

THE LIFE OF THE SPIRITUAL MAN

Now, understanding the parallel of the natural life, the elements of the life of the spiritual man can be readily grasped. Here, the seed is the life of Christ, offered as a gift from God the Father. This seed (or New Life) is sown into our natural life and is to be nurtured and educated by the Holy Spirit. However, we are not fully released into the spiritual world because our physical body has not yet been done away with. In this sense, in our earthly life, we will live a life of duality. In other words, we will live as a natural man as well as a spiritual man. Even so, our faith in Christ gives us hope that one day this duality will end and we will be fully transformed into the likeness of our Lord, Jesus Christ, and enjoy the fullness of his life and glory as a son of God.

Let's turn to some scriptures to briefly illustrate some elements of the life of the spiritual man.

JOHN 3:3-8

³ In reply Jesus declared, "I tell you the truth, no one can see the kingdom of God unless he is born again."
⁴ "How can a man be born when he is old?" Nicodemus asked. "Surely he cannot enter a second time into his mother's womb to be born!"
⁵ Jesus answered, "I tell you the truth, no one can enter the kingdom of God unless he is born of water and the Spirit. ⁶ Flesh gives birth to flesh, but the Spirit gives birth to spirit. ⁷ You should not be surprised at my saying, 'You must be born again.' ⁸ The wind blows wherever it pleases. You hear its sound, but you cannot tell where it comes from or where it is going. So it is with everyone born of the Spirit."

Here, Jesus makes it clear. Man is ordained to have natural life first and then spiritual life if he is to see and enter the Kingdom of God, or God's spiritual reality. We are born into it as spiritual babes and no amount of Bible knowledge or religious education and practice can replace or replicate this life. It is to be done solely by the Spirit of God.

We must come to God the Father in spirit and truth.

JOHN 4:23-24

²³ Yet a time is coming and has now come when the true worshipers will worship the Father in spirit and truth, for they are the kind of worshipers the Father seeks. ²⁴ God is spirit, and his worshipers must worship in spirit and in truth."

Here, the word "truth" in Greek is *aletheia*. Strong's Lexicon explains it as:

[The] truth as taught in the Christian religion, respecting God and the execution of his purposes through Christ, and respecting the duties of man, opposing alike to the superstitions of the Gentiles and the inventions of the Jews, and the corrupt opinions and precepts of false teachers even among Christians.[d]

In essence, it is the living reality of the Kingdom of God with which our spiritual life presently engages, not a distant or lofty system of thoughts or glamorous and rigid rituals that are "dead" or "unfruitful" to our present spiritual life. It is often the simple and plain things of life, those that are not appealing to man's appetites for grandeur and glory.

Jesus uses "see" and "enter" to describe the steps we are to take to be released into his Kingdom. Flesh and blood cannot accomplish this. It is only to be done by the Holy Spirit. Now, just like a nurturing and loving mother or a patient and wise teacher, the Holy Spirit will take His time to nourish, comfort, teach, and empower us into the maturity/perfection of this life. Then we can truly enjoy our freedom and fulfill our role in the Kingdom of God as a spiritual man.

JOHN 16:13–15

¹³ But when he, the Spirit of truth, comes, he will guide you into all truth. He will not speak on his own; he will speak only what he hears, and he will tell you what is yet to come. [These are primarily about the spiritual things of God's Kingdom, not the natural things

---

[d] Strong, James. *Strong's Exhaustive Concordance to the Bible.* Hendrickson Publishing, 1996.

of this world, as some would like to make it.] ¹⁴ He will bring glory to me by taking from what is mine and making it known to you. ¹⁵ All that belongs to the Father is mine. That is why I said the Spirit will take from what is mine and make it known to you.

To "see" is to have our spiritual senses opened to the spiritual reality of the Kingdom of God. To "enter" is to grow and walk in the understanding and wisdom of the Spirit. In order to attain unto these, we must be nourished with spiritual food that is suitable for the season we are in, like a baby growing into a mature man, or a seed into a fruitful tree.

SPIRITUAL FOOD

The life of Jesus is the substance of our spiritual food. Let's look at some key points.

Lesson in the Wilderness

God intended to teach the Israelites a lesson in the wilderness, which was explicitly stated by Him through Moses:

> **DEUTERONOMY 8:2-5**
> *² Remember how the Lord your God led you all the way in the desert these forty years, to humble you and to test you in order to know what was in your heart, whether or not you would keep his commands. ³ He humbled you, causing you to hunger and then feeding you with manna, which neither you nor your fathers had known, to teach you that man does not live on bread alone but on every word that comes from the mouth of the Lord. ⁴ Your clothes did not wear out and your feet did not swell during these forty years. ⁵ Know then in your heart that as a man disciplines his son, so the Lord your God disciplines you.*

God always intended to restore His way of love and wisdom to His children. He would do this by disciplining them in His ways, as a father would his son. Through His dealings with their food and water in the wilderness, He wanted the Israelites to learn that these were a means by which their spiritual eyes and ears could be opened, so that they could understand His heart and learn His ways, and thus receive His goodness (that is, His love, wisdom, and glory). We know the heartbreaking story. They hardened their hearts in disbelief and provoked God into anger, again and again, with their rebellion and stubbornness. Eventually they invoked His judgment, which was that they, as a generation, would die in the wilderness, save only a few, just as He had judged Adam and Eve in the beginning. Commenting on this, Paul says:

1 CORINTHIANS 10:1–11
[1] For I do not want you to be ignorant of the fact, brothers, that our forefathers were all under the cloud and that they all passed through the sea. [2] They were all baptized into Moses in the cloud and in the sea. [3] They all ate the same spiritual food [4] and drank the same spiritual drink; for they drank from the spiritual rock that accompanied them, and that rock was Christ. [5] Nevertheless, God was not pleased with most of them; their bodies were scattered over the desert.

[6] Now these things occurred as examples to keep us from setting our hearts on evil things as they did. [7] Do not be idolaters, as some of them were; as it is written: "The people sat down to eat and drink and got up to indulge in pagan revelry." [8] We should not commit sexual immorality, as some of them did—and in one day twenty-three thousand of them died. [9] We should not test the Lord, as some of them did—and were killed by snakes. [10] And do not grumble, as some of them did—and were killed by the destroying angel. [11] These

things happened to them as examples and were written down as warnings for us, on whom the fulfillment of the ages has come.

Jesus was also tempted in the wilderness for 40 days without bread and water. It was not merely a personal test of physical, mental, and spiritual strength or discipline. It was part of the grand work of restoration on our behalf through His sufferings in the flesh. However, Jesus didn't fall. Rather, he endured every test, even to the point of death on a cross. Thus, once for all, he destroyed the root of sin and the power of death for those who believe in his name.

HEBREWS 2:13-18
¹³ And again,
"I will put my trust in him."
And again he says,
"Here am I, and the children God has given me." ¹⁴ Since the children have flesh and blood, he too shared in their humanity so that by his death he might destroy him who holds the power of death—that is, the devil—¹⁵ and free those who all their lives were held in slavery by their fear of death. ¹⁶ For surely it is not angels he helps, but Abraham's descendants. ¹⁷ For this reason he had to be made like his brothers in every way, in order that he might become a merciful and faithful high priest in service to God, and that he might make atonement for the sins of the people. ¹⁸ Because he himself suffered when he was tempted, he is able to help those who are being tempted.

Jesus Is Our Spiritual Bread and Water

Jesus Christ is our manna from heaven and water from the rock. Let's take a look at what he said about himself:

JOHN 6:26–35

²⁶ Jesus answered, "I tell you the truth, you are looking for me, not because you saw miraculous signs but because you ate the loaves and had your fill. ²⁷ Do not work for food that spoils, but for food that endures to eternal life, which the Son of Man will give you. On him God the Father has placed his seal of approval."
²⁸ Then they asked him, "What must we do to do the works God requires?"
²⁹ Jesus answered, "The work of God is this: to believe in the one he has sent."
³⁰ So they asked him, "What miraculous sign then will you give that we may see it and believe you? What will you do? ³¹ Our forefathers ate the manna in the desert; as it is written: 'He gave them bread from heaven to eat.'"
³² Jesus said to them, "I tell you the truth, it is not Moses who has given you the bread from heaven, but it is my Father who gives you the true bread from heaven. ³³ For the bread of God is he who comes down from heaven and gives life to the world."
³⁴ "Sir," they said, "from now on give us this bread."
³⁵ Then Jesus declared, "I am the bread of life. He who comes to me will never go hungry, and he who believes in me will never be thirsty.

JOHN 4:11–14

¹¹ "Sir," the woman said, "you have nothing to draw with and the well is deep. Where can you get this living water? ¹² Are you greater than our father Jacob, who gave us the well and drank from it himself, as did also his sons and his flocks and herds?"
¹³ Jesus answered, "Everyone who drinks this water will be thirsty again, ¹⁴ but whoever drinks the water I give him will never thirst. Indeed, the water I give him will become in him a spring of water welling up to eternal life."

The Seed

It is obvious that Jesus was not talking about physical bread and water, rather, they are spiritual.

The Symbolism of Communion

This kind of food and water is only available to us by the Holy Spirit. This is what Jesus himself testified:

> **JOHN 7:37-39**
> *³⁷ On the last and greatest day of the Feast (of Tabernacle), Jesus stood and said in a loud voice, "If anyone is thirsty, let him come to me and drink. ³⁸ Whoever believes in me, as the Scripture has said, streams of living water will flow from within him." ³⁹ By this he meant the Spirit, whom those who believed in him were later to receive. Up to that time the Spirit had not been given, since Jesus had not yet been glorified.*

This glorification was his death. As the Lamb of God who was slain from the foundation of the world, he came into time and space and became a man of flesh and blood. John the Baptist testified that Jesus was the Lamb of God, who came to take away the sin of the world (John 1:29). Jesus himself explained:

> **JOHN 6:44-58**
> *⁴⁴ "No one can come to me unless the Father who sent me draws him, and I will raise him up at the last day. ⁴⁵ It is written in the Prophets: 'They will all be taught by God.' Everyone who listens to the Father and learns from him comes to me. ⁴⁶ No one has seen the Father except the one who is from God; only he has seen the Father. ⁴⁷ I tell you the truth, he who believes has everlasting life. ⁴⁸ I am the bread of life. ⁴⁹ Your forefathers ate the manna in the desert, yet they died. ⁵⁰ But here is the bread that comes down from*

heaven, which a man may eat and not die. ⁵¹ *I am the living bread that came down from heaven. If anyone eats of this bread, he will live forever. This bread is my flesh, which I will give for the life of the world."*
⁵² *Then the Jews began to argue sharply among themselves, "How can this man give us his flesh to eat?"*
⁵³ *Jesus said to them, "I tell you the truth, unless you eat the flesh of the Son of Man and drink his blood, you have no life in you.*
⁵⁴ *Whoever eats my flesh and drinks my blood has eternal life, and I will raise him up at the last day.* ⁵⁵ *For my flesh is real food and my blood is real drink.* ⁵⁶ *Whoever eats my flesh and drinks my blood remains in me, and I in him.* ⁵⁷ *Just as the living Father sent me and I live because of the Father, so the one who feeds on me will live because of me.* ⁵⁸ *This is the bread that came down from heaven. Your forefathers ate manna and died, but he who feeds on this bread will live forever."*

This, in essence, is the content of his testimony at the Last Super. Passover was ordained by God for the Israelites when He delivered them out of Egypt and should have been observed in their midst. Finally, it was fulfilled in the person of Christ Jesus, and with it, the transition from the Old Testament (covenant of the law) to the New Testament (eternal covenant).

This is the true meaning of our spiritual communion, that we partake of the bread and wine, which symbolize his body and his blood, or the wholeness of his life as the Lamb of God.

The substance is his life, which is his teaching or wisdom. However, it takes some sort of medium to convey or serve it. In this light, the written word of God, the Bible, quickened by the teachings of the Holy Spirit, often done through the ministry of the Body of Christ, is an indispensable means for the impartation of his wisdom. This impartation or service is a process like that of a child, growing through the seasons of life to be nourished into a mature man.

SPIRITUAL GROWTH AND MATURITY

It starts with milk. It may be helpful for us to know that this is actually a "big" theme in the early apostle's teachings. Let's take a look:

Peter:

1 PETER 2:1-3

¹ Therefore, rid yourselves of all malice and all deceit, hypocrisy, envy, and slander of every kind. ² Like newborn babies, crave pure spiritual milk, so that by it you may grow up in your salvation, ³ now that you have tasted that the Lord is good.

Paul:

1 CORINTHIANS 3:1-4

¹ Brothers, I could not address you as spiritual but as worldly—mere infants in Christ. ² I gave you milk, not solid food, for you were not yet ready for it. Indeed, you are still not ready. ³ You are still worldly. For since there is jealousy and quarreling among you, are you not worldly? Are you not acting like mere men? ⁴ For when one says, "I follow Paul," and another, "I follow Apollos," are you not mere men?

The Author of Hebrews:

HEBREWS 5:11-14
[11] We have much to say about this, but it is hard to explain because you are slow to learn. [12] In fact, though by this time you ought to be teachers, you need someone to teach you the elementary truths of God's word all over again. You need milk, not solid food! [13] Anyone who lives on milk, being still an infant, is not acquainted with the teaching about righteousness. [14] But solid food is for the mature, who by constant use have trained themselves to distinguish good from evil.

In the early church, it was a common practice for a set of elementary teachings to be passed on to the new believers or disciples. This task was entrusted to the apostles, prophets, and teachers, or those who had the capacity to expound on these things with a trust from the Lord and the help of the Holy Spirit. The purpose was not merely to impart knowledge, even though knowledge will be the content, but most importantly to produce a needed context for spiritual understanding and an orderly, loving, and nurturing environment for the spiritual growth of the believers. In this environment, all would be able to grow into "the full stature of Christ." Paul speaks of this:

EPHESIANS 4:11-16
[11] It was he who gave some to be apostles, some to be prophets, some to be evangelists, and some to be pastors and teachers, [12] to prepare God's people for works of service, so that the body of Christ may be built up [13] until we all reach unity in the faith and in the knowledge of the Son of God and become mature, attaining to the whole measure of the fullness of Christ.
[14] Then we will no longer be infants, tossed back and forth by the waves, and blown here and there by every wind of teaching and by

the cunning and craftiness of men in their deceitful scheming. *¹⁵ Instead, speaking the truth in love, we will in all things grow up into him who is the Head, that is, Christ. ¹⁶ From him the whole body, joined and held together by every supporting ligament, grows and builds itself up in love, as each part does its work.*

Jesus used a parable to illustrate this:

MATTHEW 24:45-51

⁴⁵ "Who then is the faithful and wise servant, whom the master has put in charge of the servants in his household to give them their food at the proper time? ⁴⁶ It will be good for that servant whose master finds him doing so when he returns. ⁴⁷ I tell you the truth, he will put him in charge of all his possessions. ⁴⁸ But suppose that servant is wicked and says to himself, 'My master is staying away a long time,' ⁴⁹ and he then begins to beat his fellow servants and to eat and drink with drunkards. ⁵⁰ The master of that servant will come on a day when he does not expect him and at an hour he is not aware of. ⁵¹ He will cut him to pieces and assign him a place with the hypocrites, where there will be weeping and gnashing of teeth.

We can observe a tree, or the life of a child, to see the process. It takes many seasons and years for a tree to grow up and to bear fruit. It takes all stages of development for a child to grow up into a strong, wise, and mature man, physically and mentally. The spiritual man takes on the same pattern. He grows into spiritual maturity.

SCRIPTURES

Spiritual Life

1 CORINTHIANS 15:35-49

35 But someone may ask, "How are the dead raised? With what kind of body will they come?" 36 How foolish! What you sow does not come to life unless it dies. 37 When you sow, you do not plant the body that will be, but just a seed, perhaps of wheat or of something else. 38 But God gives it a body as he has determined, and to each kind of seed he gives its own body. 39 All flesh is not the same: Men have one kind of flesh, animals have another, birds another and fish another. 40 There are also heavenly bodies and there are earthly bodies; but the splendor of the heavenly bodies is one kind, and the splendor of the earthly bodies is another. 41 The sun has one kind of splendor, the moon another and the stars another; and star differs from star in splendor.

42 So will it be with the resurrection of the dead. The body that is sown is perishable, it is raised imperishable; 43 it is sown in dishonor, it is raised in glory; it is sown in weakness, it is raised in power; 44 it is sown a natural body, it is raised a spiritual body.

If there is a natural body, there is also a spiritual body. 45 So it is written: "The first man Adam became a living being"; the last Adam, a life-giving spirit. 46 The spiritual did not come first, but the natural, and after that the spiritual. 47 The first man was of the dust of the earth, the second man from heaven. 48 As was the earthly man, so are those who are of the earth; and as is the man from heaven, so also are those who are of heaven. 49 And just as we have borne the likeness of the earthly man, so shall we bear the likeness of the man from heaven.

2 CORINTHIANS 4:6-7

6 For God, who said, "Let light shine out of darkness," made his light shine in our hearts to give us the light of the knowledge of the glory of God in the face of Christ. ⁷ But we have this treasure in jars of clay to show that this all-surpassing power is from God and not from us.

2 CORINTHIANS 4:16-18; 5:1-5

¹⁶ Therefore we do not lose heart. Though outwardly we are wasting away, yet inwardly we are being renewed day by day. ¹⁷ For our light and momentary troubles are achieving for us an eternal glory that far outweighs them all. ¹⁸ So we fix our eyes not on what is seen, but on what is unseen. For what is seen is temporary, but what is unseen is eternal.

¹ Now we know that if the earthly tent we live in is destroyed, we have a building from God, an eternal house in heaven, not built by human hands. ² Meanwhile we groan, longing to be clothed with our heavenly dwelling, ³ because when we are clothed, we will not be found naked. ⁴ For while we are in this tent, we groan and are burdened, because we do not wish to be unclothed but to be clothed with our heavenly dwelling, so that what is mortal may be swallowed up by life. ⁵ Now it is God who has made us for this very purpose and has given us the Spirit as a deposit, guaranteeing what is to come.

Spiritual Food and Growth

MATTHEW 16:5-12

⁵ When they went across the lake, the disciples forgot to take bread. ⁶ "Be careful," Jesus said to them. "Be on your guard against the yeast of the Pharisees and Sadducees."

⁷ They discussed this among themselves and said, "It is because we didn't bring any bread."

⁸ Aware of their discussion, Jesus asked, "You of little faith, why are you talking among yourselves about having no bread? ⁹ Do you still not understand? Don't you remember the five loaves for the five thousand, and how many basketfuls you gathered? [10] *Or the seven loaves for the four thousand, and how many basketfuls you gathered?* [11] *How is it you don't understand that I was not talking to you about bread? But be on your guard against the yeast of the Pharisees and Sadducees."* [12] *Then they understood that he was not telling them to guard against the yeast used in bread, but against the teaching of the Pharisees and Sadducees.*

1 CORINTHIANS 11:23–26

[23] *For I received from the Lord what I also passed on to you: The Lord Jesus, on the night he was betrayed, took bread,* [24] *and when he had given thanks, he broke it and said, "This is my body, which is for you; do this in remembrance of me."* [25] *In the same way, after supper he took the cup, saying, "This cup is the new covenant in my blood; do this, whenever you drink it, in remembrance of me."* [26] *For whenever you eat this bread and drink this cup, you proclaim the Lord's death until he comes.*

QUESTIONS FOR REVIEW

1. How would you compare the life of a spiritual man with that of a natural man?

2. What are your natural senses? Do you think they are comparable to your spiritual senses? If so, in what way?

3. Why did Jesus warn of the disciples of yeast in the bread?

QUESTIONS
FOR MEDITATION & APPLICATION

1. What are the stages of the growth of a natural man? Do you think they are applicable to our spiritual growth? If so, in what way?

2. Read the following parable then explain what do you think Jesus meant by this verse in Matthew 13:33?

   33 The kingdom of heaven is like yeast that a woman took and mixed into a large amount of flour until it worked all through the dough.

3. Give consideration to the effect that food has on your physical health. Do you think these effects are applicable in principle to your spiritual health? If so, how?

_____

_____

_____

4. In order to make yourself grow healthy in the spirit, what would you do to improve your spiritual lifestyle?

_____

_____

_____

7

SPIRITUAL FRUIT AND SPIRITUAL GIFTS

OVERVIEW

In this chapter, we will continue to discuss other important aspects of the spiritual life:

- Spiritual Fruit
- Spiritual Gifts

SPIRITUAL FRUIT

In the last chapter, we mentioned spiritual growth as a process, and spiritual maturity as the fulfillment of the life God gives to us.

A tree takes time to develop from being a seed to becoming a full-grown tree, and then it is able to bear fruit. Now, for a farmer, the most fulfilling moment of his labor is when he has harvested the fruit from the tree. God is the Master Farmer or the Great Gardener, and He takes good care of us, always working to see that we become a tree full of good fruits.

What is Spiritual Fruit?

Paul mentions nine types of spiritual fruit in his letter to the Galatians:

> **GALATIANS 5:22–23**
> *²² But the fruit of the Spirit is love, joy, peace, patience, kindness, goodness, faithfulness, ²³ gentleness and self-control. Against such things there is no law.*

It is easy to see that all these attributes are characteristics of a person, describing the qualities of God's personality. Evidently, God is more interested in who we are in Him than what we can do for Him.

Two lives are contrasted here. One life is like that of a Gentile indulging in the evil desires that were the norm of the secular culture of the Roman world. The other life is like that of a Jew under the law, zealously trying to fulfill the righteous requirements of God by his own endeavors. Neither is the life that Paul was trying to share with others. The life he envisions is for one to live by the Spirit, and to allow God to work out His life in us through our faith and obedience to Christ Jesus.

> **"God is more interested in who we are in Him than what we can do for Him."**

By following different ways of life, we will bear different kinds of spiritual fruits. We reap what we sow. If we diligently seek the life of Jesus Christ and the righteousness that comes from his Kingdom, we will grow into eternal life and bear everlasting fruits. We will become the glory and the joy of our heavenly Father.

MATTHEW 6:33

[33] But seek first his kingdom and his righteousness, and all these things will be given to you as well.

The kingdom mentioned here is our spiritual life in and of God the Father, which is vested in His spiritual reality. It is a spiritual kingdom of His power, glory, order, righteousness, and majesty. As we grow and partake of His divine nature, we will become more and more like Him who is love, peace, righteousness, joy, justice, mercy, goodness, etc. Paul mentions this in the book of Romans:

ROMANS 14:17

[17] For the kingdom of God is not a matter of eating and drinking, but of righteousness, peace and joy in the Holy Spirit,

We can see that life in the Kingdom of God is not about external achievements for God, rather the inner spiritual life in Him, which is to bear spiritual fruit. Please take note, the eating and drinking mentioned here is not referring to personal eating habits. Paul used it to illustrate the kind of fellowship the believers in Rome indulged in. Evidently, they had drifted far away from the practice and substance of true fellowship or communion in Christ Jesus. In Paul's mind, fellowship or communion in Christ was not about external behaviors or rituals, but about the partaking of the substance of the life of Christ. It should be done in conformity with the spiritual reality issued from the Kingdom of God.

They were to fellowship and partake in spiritual things together in the order of the Kingdom, with reverence and understanding.

How to Bear Spiritual Fruit

How do we bear fruit? Jesus' teachings are very clear about this: abide in him.

> **JOHN 15:1-8**
> *¹ "I am the true vine, and my Father is the gardener. ² He cuts off every branch in me that bears no fruit, while every branch that does bear fruit he prunes so that it will be even more fruitful. ³ You are already clean because of the word I have spoken to you. ⁴ Remain in me, and I will remain in you. No branch can bear fruit by itself; it must remain in the vine. Neither can you bear fruit unless you remain in me.*
> *⁵ "I am the vine; you are the branches. If a man remains in me and I in him, he will bear much fruit; apart from me you can do nothing.*

> *⁶ If anyone does not remain in me, he is like a branch that is thrown away and withers; such branches are picked up, thrown into the fire and burned. ⁷ If you remain in me and my words remain in you, ask whatever you wish, and it will be given you. ⁸ This is to my Father's glory, that you bear much fruit, showing yourselves to be my disciples.*

Let us give some key observations of this very important passage relating to our spiritual life. As His servants, we are the collaborative work (handiwork) of the Father, Son, and Spirit.

God the Father is the gardener or the vine-dresser. This means that He alone sets the standard by which the quality of the fruits is judged, whether good or bad. He will also prune the vine so that it will bear good fruit.

Jesus Christ is the vine. He is the source of all nourishment. Only through abiding in the vine can any branch bear fruit.

We are the branches, and are given life in the vine, so that we will bear much fruit. We can only do so if we remain in the vine. That is our life by the power of the Holy Spirit and by faith in Christ Jesus.

How do we abide in him? He gives clear instruction in the following passage:

JOHN 15:9–17

> *⁹ "As the Father has loved me, so have I loved you. Now remain in my love. ¹⁰ If you obey my commands, you will remain in my love, just as I have obeyed my Father's commands and remain in his love.*

¹¹ I have told you this so that my joy may be in you and that your joy may be complete. ¹² My command is this: Love each other as I have loved you. ¹³ Greater love has no one than this, that he lay down his life for his friends. ¹⁴ You are my friends if you do what I command. ¹⁵ I no longer call you servants, because a servant does not know his master's business. Instead, I have called you friends, for everything that I learned from my Father I have made known to you. ¹⁶ You did not choose me, but I chose you and appointed you to go and bear fruit—fruit that will last. Then the Father will give you whatever you ask in my name. ¹⁷ This is my command: Love each other.

Godly Love is Our Best Spiritual Fruit and Service

Remain in His love and love one another—this will show the world that we are His disciples. How liberating and illuminating to see that He is not keen to have us to perform miracles and signs (which are more related to the working out of our gifts by the Holy Spirit). Rather, he would have His heart of love in us, and extend that love to others, especially those within His Family. Let's pause and ponder on this for a moment, because it portrays a fundamentally different picture of how we are to relate to one another, and live together as the people of God compared to the many norms and ideas of modern Christianity. Indeed, when perfection or maturity comes (which is godly love) the childish things should be done away with. In the above passage, Jesus spoke about our spiritual maturation and the production of spiritual fruit. Later, Paul expounded on this topic as well.

1 CORINTHIANS 13:1-13

¹ If I speak in the tongues of men and of angels, but have not love, I am only a resounding gong or a clanging cymbal. ² *If I have the gift of prophecy and can fathom all mysteries and all knowledge, and if I have a faith that can move mountains, but have not love, I am nothing.* ³ *If I give all I possess to the poor and surrender my body to the flames, but have not love, I gain nothing.*

⁴ *Love is patient, love is kind. It does not envy, it does not boast, it is not proud.* ⁵ *It is not rude, it is not self-seeking, it is not easily angered, it keeps no record of wrongs.* ⁶ *Love does not delight in evil but rejoices with the truth.* ⁷ *It always protects, always trusts, always hopes, always perseveres.*

⁸ *Love never fails. But where there are prophecies, they will cease; where there are tongues, they will be stilled; where there is knowledge, it will pass away.* ⁹ *For we know in part and we prophesy in part,* ¹⁰ *but when perfection comes, the imperfect disappears.* ¹¹ *When I was a child, I talked like a child, I thought like a child, I reasoned like a child. When I became a man, I put childish ways behind me.* ¹² *Now we see but a poor reflection as in a mirror; then we shall see face to face. Now I know in part; then I shall know fully, even as I am fully known.* ¹³ *And now these three remain: faith, hope and love. But the greatest of these is love.*

This is the "discipleship," or the business of the Father that the Lord Jesus revealed and entrusted to the early apostles. Now we see that the Lord taught and "sent them" so that they could co-labor with him, in and by the Holy Spirit, in order to produce a culture of love in the Household of God, different from the culture of this world. They were to serve others in the way that he had served them. In essence, he entrusted them to teach others how to love as God would have them love. The true content of discipleship goes far beyond just having people saved by receiving the gospel and the Lord. Rather, it is to teach others how to love with wisdom and understanding in the Household of God.

Today, we often hear about the "power of God" as being demonstrated through the gifts, or the so-called "anointing" of a person or ministry. This has created a picture or an ideal model of what it means to be "sent" by God. Because of this, the current culture or movement of the Kingdom of God seems to focus mainly on the manifestation of spiritual gifts. This is such a short-sighted (if not wrong) vision or pattern of the culture of the Kingdom of God. God does give us great gifts, but these gifts are given for a specific purpose. This purpose is to build up His Household, and to serve the fellowship or communion of Christ therein. This is the way and power of His love, and the "impartation" of His wisdom.

> **"The true content of discipleship...is to teach others how to love with wisdom and understanding in the Household of God."**

On one hand, the Lord's command to love one another is not a religious creed that confines or demands one to do good deeds, or to simply seek the harmony of man (Jesus called this, "the peace of the world"). This was the content of the Jews' teachings in Jesus' time, and Jesus was not in agreement with such teachings. In fact, he criticized the Jews as practicing hypocrisy—honoring God with their lips, but not with their hearts. Rather, Jesus' intention was to write his law of love on men's hearts and minds so that they could become like him; sons that belong to and are taught by their heavenly Father, and that are endowed with His wisdom and love.

On the other hand, the exercise, practice, and learning of His way of love is entrusted to the Church as God's Family on earth as it is in heaven. In essence, the business of the Father is to have his heavenly Family, including those who believe on the name of Jesus Christ, grow into His culture and order that comes from above, and not to mingle with the culture or wisdom from below—which is earthly, demonic, and sensual, as James put it. By this, they can all grow and become His mature sons, "like the Son of God."

This was always the design or vision with which the Father had positioned and blessed man when He first created him. Man was to multiply and fill the earth as a special race, one that is taught by God and able to represent Him in every way. Man was to serve Him and be a conduit of His love and wisdom (which is His glory) unto all creation. For this reason, He sent His only begotten Son to become a man full of grace and truth. The Son knows the Father perfectly and is the exact image of the Father. That is, he represents His Father perfectly in His likeness. Jesus was sent by the Father to teach or to show man "the way" of life in God. It was lost when Adam and Eve sinned or missed the mark of God's divine purpose. Jesus came so that man could be restored to the desire and the ways of his heavenly Father. Father God wants to share His love and wisdom with all who belong to Him. This is the true ministry (service, work, or business of the Father) that was given to the Son. Then this ministry was given from Him to the apostles, and to us today.

In this sense, the way of godly love and godly wisdom is the true content of "the New Covenant ministry," and the real purpose of all the services that are to be rendered therein.

No wonder the Lord explained this culture of love to his disciples in this way, "The world will know you are my disciples by the way you love one other." As mentioned before, we are destined to grow into this perfect love of God by partaking in the life of the Son of God, and this with the help of His blessed and foreordained family on earth as it is in Heaven.

Abiding in Him is not simply being "filled by the Spirit," which we will never despise. Rather, and more importantly, we are to learn the Father's business or His work. That is, we are to receive godly wisdom so that we can all mature into godly love. This will confer to us a culture and a people of His own, one that is patterned after his heavenly Family and empowered by his Kingdom. This is the true meaning of what it means to be set apart or made holy, or to be called out from this evil and corrupt world into his wonderful Kingdom and Family. In this way, we become His chosen people.

> **"The symbolic meaning of the cross is the death to our old nature and life in God."**

Now, it is important for us to understand the "work of the cross" in the context of our spiritual journey in the life of Christ. The symbolic meaning of the cross is the death to our old nature and life in God. In this light, "suffering in Christ" is the working of

God's discipline unto us as sons of God and should always be emphasized.

SPIRITUAL GIFTS

For us to grow, the Lord not only gives each believer the indwelling of the Holy Spirit, but He also blesses us with gifts of the Holy Spirit in the Body of Christ or the Church. These are to be exercised out of love unto one another, so that our lives can be merged into the work or business of our heavenly Father as an expression of His life to benefit all members of His Family, and then to all creation. Whether in the receiving or the offering, we need to ask for and discern the effectiveness and the heart behind the working of spiritual gifts. Even when one is offering from a heart of sincerity and goodwill, we still need the Lord to affirm whether they are properly offered or suitable for our needs or not.

In this, godly love is the sure mark. The Lord has one standard for this love to be expressed: it is to be founded upon the reality that one has indeed laid down his or her life for others. Self-indulgence and complacency need to be purged before we can wisely and effectively exercise our spiritual gifts. Sadly, this often isn't the case within the Body of Christ today, which makes the understanding and discernment of such things even more necessary.

Now, in the Body of Christ, God gives diverse gifts to different members of the body to help each other to grow spiritually. Let's look at these gifts.

1 CORINTHIANS 12:4-11

⁴ There are different kinds of gifts, but the same Spirit. ⁵ There are different kinds of service, but the same Lord. ⁶ There are different kinds of working, but the same God works all of them in all men. ⁷ Now to each one the manifestation of the Spirit is given for the common good. ⁸ To one there is given through the Spirit the message of wisdom, to another the message of knowledge by means of the same Spirit, ⁹ to another faith by the same Spirit, to another gifts of healing by that one Spirit, ¹⁰ to another miraculous powers, to another prophecy, to another distinguishing between spirits, to another speaking in different kinds of tongues, and to still another the interpretation of tongues. ¹¹ All these are the work of one and the same Spirit, and he gives them to each one, just as he determines.

All gifts are for service, that is, to serve the members of the body, so that each member can grow, and as a result, the whole body will grow.

1 CORINTHIANS 12:27-31

²⁷ Now you are the body of Christ, and each one of you is a part of it. ²⁸ And in the church God has appointed first of all apostles, second prophets, third teachers, then workers of miracles, also those having gifts of healing, those able to help others, those with gifts of administration, and those speaking in different kinds of tongues. ²⁹ Are all apostles? Are all prophets? Are all teachers? Do all work miracles? ³⁰ Do all have gifts of healing? Do all speak in tongues? Do all interpret? ³¹ But eagerly desire the greater gifts.

And now I will show you the most excellent way.

Here Paul offers another list of spiritual gifts where he is more concerned with the persons who exercise them, rather than the manifestations of the gifts.

There is a reason that this list is in sequential order. It is partly because there are greater gifts such as apostolic and prophetic gifts, but mostly it is because this is how a local church would grow under his ministry. Paul traveled to a place and preached the gospel. Then the prophets, like Barnabas, would co-labor with him to lay down the spiritual foundation in the lives of the believers and set the order of the local church as a genuine Family of God's people—able to live together in love, faith, and freedom by the Holy Spirit. As other members of the church were baptized in the Holy Spirit, their spiritual gifts would manifest. Then they would guide those who are so gifted to practice and foster them in an orderly and helpful manner in their daily fellowships. This was a very common thing, not a scarce commodity as we commonly witness in many of today's "fellowships." In addition, the gifts were not the center of their fellowship either. The central focus was the teaching of the Word of God and the mutual help and care of one another.

Just as it is in our natural life, we enjoy and admire various talents and gifts in people. Some develop very well in life, while others don't necessarily have the chance to develop. For example, I may have a wonderful gift in music, but without the proper training and education my talent will not have the opportunity to achieve excellence. Even if I did, I would still have to decide how I should use it. Should I use it just to gain money and fame, to entertain people, or to help others? These aspects are not confined by the perfecting and using of the gift itself, but rather are decided by the purpose and value that it is used for. This always has to do with the attitude and desire of one's heart. For example, considering whether or not I have good, even the best, intentions for others in mind when using my gifts.

It is the same with our spiritual gifts. A spiritual gift is given to us by God. It needs to be stewarded, developed, and exercised for the benefit of His Kingdom, to serve Him and His people. That is why Paul continued to speak of "a more excellent way."

That more excellent way is godly love.

Let's look at a passage that clearly states how gifts are meant to serve the growth of the body, the end of which is to bear spiritual fruit and to come to spiritual maturity.

EPHESIANS 4:7–16

7 But to each one of us grace has been given as Christ apportioned it.
8 This is why it says:
"When he ascended on high, he led captives in his train and gave gifts to men."
9 (What does "he ascended" mean except that he also descended to the lower, earthly regions? 10 He who descended is the very one who ascended higher than all the heavens, in order to fill the whole universe.) 11 It was he who gave some to be apostles, some to be prophets, some to be evangelists, and some to be pastors and teachers, 12 to prepare God's people for works of service, so that the body of Christ may be built up 13 until we all reach unity in the faith and in the knowledge of the Son of God and become mature, attaining to the whole measure of the fullness of Christ.
14 Then we will no longer be infants, tossed back and forth by the waves, and blown here and there by every wind of teaching and by the cunning and craftiness of men in their deceitful scheming.
15 Instead, speaking the truth in love, we will in all things grow up

into him who is the Head, that is, Christ. ¹⁶ From him the whole body, joined and held together by every supporting ligament, grows and builds itself up in love, as each part does its work.

SCRIPTURES

Spiritual Fruit

ISAIAH 11:1-3

¹ A shoot will come up from the stump of Jesse; from his roots a Branch will bear fruit. ² The Spirit of the Lord will rest on him—the Spirit of wisdom and of understanding, the Spirit of counsel and of power, the Spirit of knowledge and of the fear of the Lord— ³ and he will delight in the fear of the Lord. He will not judge by what he sees with his eyes, or decide by what he hears with his ears;

GALATIANS 6:7-10

⁷ Do not be deceived: God cannot be mocked. A man reaps what he sows. ⁸ The one who sows to please his sinful nature, from that nature will reap destruction; the one who sows to please the Spirit, from the Spirit will reap eternal life. ⁹ Let us not become weary in doing good, for at the proper time we will reap a harvest if we do not give up. ¹⁰ Therefore, as we have opportunity, let us do good to all people, especially to those who belong to the family of believers.

JAMES 3:17-18

¹⁷ But the wisdom that comes from heaven is first of all pure; then peace-loving, considerate, submissive, full of mercy and good fruit, impartial and sincere. ¹⁸ Peacemakers who sow in peace raise a harvest of righteousness.

PSALM 1:1-3

*¹ Blessed is the man
who does not walk in the counsel of the wicked*

or stand in the way of sinners
or sit in the seat of mockers.
² But his delight is in the law of the Lord,
and on his law he meditates day and night.
³ He is like a tree planted by streams of water,
which yields its fruit in season
and whose leaf does not wither.
Whatever he does prospers.

Spiritual Gifts

ROMANS 12:3–8

³ For by the grace given me I say to every one of you: Do not think of yourself more highly than you ought, but rather think of yourself with sober judgment, in accordance with the measure of faith God has given you. ⁴ Just as each of us has one body with many members, and these members do not all have the same function, ⁵ so in Christ we who are many form one body, and each member belongs to all the others. ⁶ We have different gifts, according to the grace given us. If a man's gift is prophesying, let him use it in proportion to his faith. ⁷ If it is serving, let him serve; if it is teaching, let him teach; ⁸ if it is encouraging, let him encourage; if it is contributing to the needs of others, let him give generously; if it is leadership, let him govern diligently; if it is showing mercy, let him do it cheerfully.

1 TIMOTHY 4:14–15

¹⁴ Do not neglect your gift, which was given you through a prophetic message when the body of elders laid their hands on you.
¹⁵ Be diligent in these matters; give yourself wholly to them, so that everyone may see your progress.

2 TIMOTHY 1:6–7

⁶ *For this reason I remind you to fan into flame the gift of God, which is in you through the laying on of my hands.* ⁷ *For God did not give us a spirit of timidity, but a spirit of power, of love and of self-discipline.*

QUESTIONS FOR REVIEW

1. What do all spiritual fruit have in common?

___

___

___

2. What is the relationship between spiritual growth and spiritual fruit?

___

___

___

3. How do we grow in our spiritual life in terms of bearing fruit?

___

___

4. What are spiritual gifts? Can you make a list of them?

5. Explain spiritual gifts in the context of serving the Body of Christ.

QUESTIONS
FOR MEDITATION & APPLICATION

1. What is the relationship between spiritual fruit and spiritual gifts?

2. What do you think the role of God the Father, God the Son, and God the Holy Spirit is in the maturing of your spiritual life?

3. What are the most valuable spiritual fruit to you? Why?

_____

_____

4. What are the most valuable natural gifts you have? How can you use them?

_____

_____

_____

5. What are the most valuable spiritual gifts you have? How can you use them?

_____

_____

_____

8

THREE COMPARTMENTS OF MAN AND THE WORK OF SANCTIFICATION

OVERVIEW

In this chapter, we will consider what it means to be created in God's image, and how God designed for man to be progressively transformed into His likeness.

- Created in God's Image: Spirit, Soul, and Body
- The Work of Sanctification

In earlier chapters, we discussed the idea that God created man in His image. Man was endowed with the full capacity, both natural and spiritual, to be changed from glory to glory—even into the likeness of God.

When Adam and Eve fell, they lost the privilege of fellowship with God, and were unable to walk in His presence anymore. They lost their chance to grow in a relationship with God as their Father.

When Christ Jesus came as the Son of God, he restored the Spirit of sonship to us as his disciples, those who have been born again in him. He restored everything to us concerning our wellbeing in God the Father.

Through the Son, we are able to approach the Father.

> **2 CORINTHIANS 3:16–18**
> *16 But whenever anyone turns to the Lord, the veil is taken away. 17 Now the Lord is the Spirit, and where the Spirit of the Lord is, there is freedom. 18 And we, who with unveiled faces all reflect the Lord's glory, are being transformed into his likeness with ever-increasing glory, which comes from the Lord, who is the Spirit.*

THREE COMPARTMENTS OF MAN

Now let us look at how God created man: the composition of man.

> **GENESIS 2:7**
> *7 Then the Lord God formed the man from the dust of the*

> *ground and breathed into his nostrils the breath of life, and the man became a living being.*

This scripture explicitly states that there were three steps, or works, of God in creating Man.

The Body or Flesh of Man

The body was formed from dust. This is "the flesh," or the physical part of a human being. This should not be understood as if it were a literal pile of dirt. Rather, the flesh of man is of such a delicate design that only the Almighty would know how to use water (over 65% in an adult male, 60% in a female) and some chemicals and minerals to create an organic, living, being. Not to mention His creative design within the many specific functions of the various parts of the body.

The Spirit or Breath of Life

The breath is the spiritual part of a human being. This breath is none other than the very breath of God, which is a life-giving spirit. God the Father planted the seed of sonship in Adam and Eve when He created them.

For man, one of the great privileges of being able to fellowship with God the Father was to be taught by Him. This privilege was not granted to any other created being. It was lost when man sinned, but restored by Christ Jesus, the Son of God, as prophesied by Jeremiah.

> **JEREMIAH 31:31–34**
> *³¹ "The time is coming," declares the Lord, "when I will make a*

new covenant with the house of Israel and with the house of Judah.
³² It will not be like the covenant I made with their forefathers when I took them by the hand to lead them out of Egypt, because they broke my covenant, though I was a husband to them," declares the Lord.
³³ "This is the covenant I will make with the house of Israel after that time," declares the Lord. "I will put my law in their minds and write it on their hearts. I will be their God, and they will be my people.
³⁴ No longer will a man teach his neighbor, or a man his brother, saying, 'Know the Lord,' because they will all know me, from the least of them to the greatest," declares the Lord. "For I will forgive their wickedness and will remember their sins no more."

This is also what the apostle John spoke of when he said that those who are born of God have the right to become children of God.

What God breathed into man was the human spirit. This spirit was destined to become the dwelling place for God's Spirit, the Spirit of sonship, and the power of eternal life in Him.

This was mentioned by Paul when he said that those born of God are sealed by the Holy Spirit, as a deposit towards the fulfillment of God's promise given through His Son, Jesus Christ. This is none other than the sealing of the eternal covenant of which we are a beneficiary (as mentioned in Hebrews). This seal guarantees what is to come, even the fullness of the life of God and His glory.

This is the essence of the life of faith in Christ Jesus, who dwells in those who are "born from above." He becomes the substance of their faith, "the hope of glory." Through Him the grace or power of God for eternal life becomes available, even presently. In the "Complete Word Study Dictionary: Old Testament," Warren Baker explains:

> The human spirit and the Spirit of God are closely linked with moral character and moral attributes. God will give His people a new spirit so they will follow His decrees and laws (Ezekiel 11:19; 36:26).
>
> God's Spirit will rest on His people, transforming them (Isaiah 59:21). The Lord preserves those who have heavy spirits and broken hearts (Psalm 34:18[19]; Isaiah 65:14).
>
> The human spirit is sometimes depicted as the seat of emotion, the mind, and the will. In a song of praise, Isaiah asserted that the spirit desires the Lord (Isaiah 26:9; Job 7:11). The spirit imparts wisdom for understanding (Exodus 28:3; Deuteronomy 34:9); and carrying out one's responsibilities. David prayed for a willing spirit to aid him (Exodus 35:21; Psalm 51:10[12]).
>
> The spirit made flesh alive and is the life force of living humans and animals. The Lord makes the spirits of people that give them life (Zechariah 12:1). This spirit is from God and leaves at death (Genesis 6:3; Psalm 78:39; Ecclesiastes 3:21). The spirit is pictured as giving animation, agitation, or liveliness; the Queen of Sheba was overcome in her spirit when she saw the splendors of Solomon's world (1 Kings 10:5). Not to

have any spirit is to lose all courage; the Amorite kings had no spirit in them when they learned how Israel had crossed the Jordan. To be short of spirit is to be despondent or impatient (Ecclesiastes 6:9).

The word also describes the breath of a human being or the natural wind that blows.[e]

The Soul

Now, in the Hebrew language, this word "soul" also means "breath," the inner being of man with his thoughts and emotions. Much lies in the difference between a man's soul and his "spirit." As some put it, the soul is a self-consciousness, while, the spirit is a God-consciousness. The soul is the natural faculty and capacity of the natural man in relation to his five senses, mind, and heart that were given by God to enable him to experience the visible or natural world. The spirit is the spiritual faculty and capacity of the spiritual man in relation to his spiritual senses, mind, and heart (comparable to the natural ones) that was given by God so that man could experience the invisible or spiritual world.

The natural world is governed by natural laws or principles which are balanced by a natural order. The spiritual world is more complicated, as it includes not only the eternal realm of God, but also the angelic realm in the heavenly places. There are three heavens in existence as of this age, which can be

---

[e] Baker, Warren, and Eugene E. Carpenter. *The Complete Word Study Dictionary: Old Testament*. AMG, 2003.

compared to the three courts in the Temple and the three compartments of man. With this in mind, we will now begin to discuss a very intriguing topic: Sanctification.

THE WORK OF SANCTIFICATION

1 THESSALONIANS 5:23
²³ May God himself, the God of peace, sanctify you through and through. May your whole spirit, soul and body be kept blameless at the coming of our Lord Jesus Christ.

To sanctify something is to perform a cleansing work on or in it. This word is often translated into other phrases in the Bible such as transformation, the renewal of the mind by the Holy Spirit, purification as in the example of gold, the baptisms of water, fire, and the Holy Spirit, the testing and proving of our faith, sufferings in Christ, etc. These are the terms used to emphasize a certain aspect of the same thing.

Simply put, sanctification is the process whereby a believer in Christ is transformed into the likeness of God, and brought under the governance of the Lord Jesus, into the will of God.

This is a process or work wrought by the Holy Spirit, who perfects all things. It begins in the innermost being of a man which is his spirit, then it proceeds to the soul, and finally to the body. This reality that is initiated and accomplished within the believer is foreshadowed by the temple in the Old Testament. The temple was made up of the Holy of Holies, the Inner Court, and the Outer Court. (For more details, please refer to the Old Testament, where the requirements for how one is to enter the Temple of God, and the way the priests are to cleanse the Temple are illustrated.) It will manifest itself as a spiritual reality with discernible and substantial changes after it flows from the inner most part of the man, to his soul, and then to his body. The Spirit will sanctify the man through and through to make him pure and blameless before the Lord.

This process can take a lifetime. It many times is compared to the process by which gold is refined by fire. The dross and impurities are burned away in order to produce pure gold. Actually, we should know that God honored gold above all other metals because He created it with the purpose of showing how a man is sanctified, and thus proven, and then set apart as holy. Anything that does not submit to this process of sanctification will be burned away, so that only what is pure and holy will remain.

By the same token, we could say that sanctification is the process of producing the fullness of Christ in us. It will bring about the Mind of Christ in a man. A man is matured in God's sight when he has the Mind of Christ, and this certainly takes time.

God has designed it to be so. The Father ordained this to be an integral part of a son's life, through which he would perfect him into the life of Christ. In this way, a son's life can even be the pattern (or standard of) how He intended to show us Himself, in all truth and grace. The Son is the exact representation, or reflection, of the Father.

The process begins with learning to be governed by the Holy Spirit. This is done through the process of yielding to the leading of the Spirit and to His governance on our part. An infant does not reflect the character of the Father in the beginning. However, over time, as he matures as a son, he will be able to do so. As you become acquainted with the ways of the Spirit, the Father and the Son will be revealed. Your life will be revealed in the glory of God as He approves your righteousness in Christ.

The glory of God has substance and weight. When our heart is right and truly desires the Lord, the Spirit will come to rest upon us in His glory. Then we become, in reality, the dwelling place of God. The Spirit does not yield to the interests or ways of man, and will bring about spiritual discipline in order to produce the necessary result of sanctification, our holiness in Christ. This is done in love, and is used to build up the Son into all righteousness.

God's glory is invisible, and we are created as a vessel of His glory. It is His desire for us to be filled with the fullness of His life in Christ Jesus. This begins with having Jesus Christ as the foundation of our spiritual life. When this is firmly established, we will not be easily swayed by the evil desires of our old carnal life, or by the schemes of the evil one. Just like the Tabernacle had to be built according to the pattern given by God in order for His visible glory to come down, so too our spiritual temple must be built according to the pattern life of Christ Jesus as a son of God, in order for His invisible glory to dwell in us. As the workmanship of God, we are not only living stones in the temple of the Lord in which His Spirit dwells, but we are to become the very temple of God.

Paul put it this way:

COLOSSIANS 2:6–10

⁶ So then, just as you received Christ Jesus as Lord, continue to live in him, ⁷ rooted and built up in him, strengthened in the faith as you were taught, and overflowing with thankfulness.

⁸ See to it that no one takes you captive through hollow and deceptive philosophy, which depends on human tradition and the basic principles of this world rather than on Christ.

⁹ For in Christ all the fullness of the Deity lives in bodily form, ¹⁰ and you have been given fullness in Christ, who is the head over every power and authority.

SCRIPTURES

Three Compartments of Man

ZECHARIAH 12:1
¹ A prophesy: The word of the Lord concerning Israel. The Lord, who stretches out the heavens, who lays the foundation of the earth, and who forms the spirit of man within him, declares:

ECCLESIASTES 12:7
⁷ and the dust returns to the ground it came from, and the spirit returns to God who gave it.

ISAIAH 59:21
²¹ "As for me, this is my covenant with them," says the Lord. "My Spirit, who is on you, and my words that I have put in your mouth will not depart from your mouth, or from the mouths of your children, or from the mouths of their descendants from this time on and forever," says the Lord.

EZEKIEL 37:5
⁵ This is what the Sovereign Lord says to these bones: I will make breath enter you, and you will come to life.

Sanctification

JOHN 17:16-19
¹⁶ They are not of the world, even as I am not of it. ¹⁷ Sanctify them by the truth; your word is truth. ¹⁸ As you sent me into the world, I have sent them into the world. ¹⁹ For them I sanctify myself, that they too may be truly sanctified.

ACTS 26:18

18 to open their eyes and turn them from darkness to light, and from the power of Satan to God, so that they may receive forgiveness of sins and a place among those who are sanctified by faith in me.'

EPHESIANS 5:26–27

26 [Christ] to make her [the Church] holy, cleansing her by the washing with water through the word, 27 and to present her to himself as a radiant church, without stain or wrinkle or any other blemish, but holy and blameless.

HEBREWS 9:13–14

13 The blood of goats and bulls and the ashes of a heifer sprinkled on those who are ceremonially unclean sanctify them so that they are outwardly clean. 14 How much more, then, will the blood of Christ, who through the eternal Spirit offered himself unblemished to God, cleanse our consciences from acts that lead to death, so that we may serve the living God!

QUESTIONS FOR REVIEW

1. List some observations concerning the Spirit of God and the Spirit of Man.

2. How did sin affect man in the three parts of his being?

3. What is the foundation for our sanctification as a believer of Christ? How so?

4. We have mentioned two ways of thinking in the past: eternal and linear. How does this apply to sanctification?

_____

_____

_____

QUESTIONS
FOR MEDITATION & APPLICATION

1. You may have had previous ideas of what being human means before you knew the Lord. Do you have a different opinion after reading this chapter? Why?

___

___

___

2. What should you do in order to cooperate with the work of sanctification by the Holy Spirit?

___

___

___

3. Why should you keep yourself holy in such contexts?

- Being the temple of the Holy Spirit

___

- Waiting for the coming of the Lord

9

DISCIPLINED INTO HOLINESS

OVERVIEW

In this chapter, we will discuss spiritual discipline, and how it complements the work of sanctification:

- Sanctification and Discipline
- Discipleship and Discipline
- The Father's Discipline to a Son
- Self-Discipline and Discipline within God's Family
- Holiness

In the last chapter, we discussed the work of sanctification. The Holy Spirit, given to us by God, will initiate and fulfill the process of the sanctification of our spirit, soul, and body, making us to be without spot or blemish in the day of the Lord, suitable to be His Bride. However, there is another very important process working in parallel which is to learn the discipline of the Lord. In this work, we are required to be amenable and obedient to the will and ways of our heavenly Father and of the Lord Jesus Christ.

SANCTIFICATION AND DISCIPLINE

Sanctification is a work reserved solely for God Himself, so that no one can claim credit for doing anything by his or her own merit.

However, as with many things in the work of God, He uses the agents of His choice to accomplish His intended purpose through the relationships and circumstances that He foreordains.

The work of sanctification by the Spirit is directly connected to and accomplished by a process of discipline, whether imposed or inspired.

By saying imposed, we mean that an external agent, consciously or unconsciously, is used by God to impose disciplines of various kinds in order to accomplish His intentions. This external agent, many times is an individual sent by, or used in, God's grace. However, this "right to discipline" can be abused or usurped to cause unbalanced and unnecessary consequences in our lives (for example, when a child is mistreated by an adult).

By saying inspired, we mean that our own consciousness will be convicted of our improper intentions, desires, or actions through the power of the Holy Spirit. We then will be able to repent from unrighteousness and disobedience.

DISCIPLESHIP AND DISCIPLINE

As previously discussed, God's intention for man before the Fall was that He would walk with him and impart His wisdom and nature to him, thereby transforming him from His image into His likeness. This is the pattern after which Jesus walked with his disciples while on earth. Jesus commissioned them to teach and replicate this pattern—or, make disciples. He gave his disciples all authority and power, enabling them to overcome the enemy and to co-labor with him to see the restoration of all his promises for those who choose to believe in his name.

> **MATTHEW 28:18-20**
> *[18] Then Jesus came to them and said, "All authority in heaven and on earth has been given to me. [19] Therefore go and make disciples of all nations, baptizing them in the name of the Father and of the Son and of the Holy Spirit, [20] and teaching them to obey everything I have commanded you. And surely I am with you always, to the very end of the age."*

Sadly, somehow through the Church Age, this great commission changed into merely making converts, and became something far removed from the true nature of discipleship. Spiritual life was substituted with religious formula. God's wisdom was replaced by intellectual education. Kingdom reality was made to be either a mystical dream world, or reduced and tweaked to validate worldly happiness and pragmatic needs of man. The hope and pursuit of the glory of God was changed into the competition and exaltation of the glory of man. The culture of the Family or the Household of God was changed into man-made traditions for religious duties and activities. Darkness yet again veiled man's mind, and a spiritual life of abundance was forsaken. Without the Spirit of God, what is man? Is he not the dry bones in the valley of darkness (Ezekiel 37:1–14)?

True spiritual teaching is not just an intellectual lesson of casual learning or an informal discussion. It is uniquely tailored for a son of God, by the one who is the King of kings and Lord of lords. It can be likened to a king of righteousness and justice training the heir to his throne. The prince is to be put into the best hands and to be taught all things concerning the governing of the kingdom. Moreover, he is to learn his father's character—to love righteousness and hate evil, and to have mercy and compassion on his subjects. It is in this light that Christ Jesus, the Son, teaches us about his Father. This is how he revealed the Father's name to his disciples. We call this kind of wisdom Kingly Wisdom. With it, Jesus Christ, the Lion of Judah, rules his Father's Kingdom with an iron scepter.

HEBREWS 2:11–12

[11] Both the one who makes men holy and those who are made holy are of the same family. So Jesus is not ashamed to call them brothers. [12] He says,
"I will declare your name to my brothers;

in the presence of the congregation I will sing your praises."

JOHN 16:25-28
[25] "Though I have been speaking figuratively, a time is coming when I will no longer use this kind of language but will tell you plainly about my Father. [26] In that day you will ask in my name. I am not saying that I will ask the Father on your behalf. [27] No, the Father himself loves you because you have loved me and have believed that I came from God. [28] I came from the Father and entered the world; now I am leaving the world and going back to the Father."

JOHN 17:26
[26] I have made you known to them, and will continue to make you known in order that the love you have for me may be in them and that I myself may be in them."

KINGLY WISDOM	PRIESTLY WISDOM
The son shows and teaches the nature of the Father's heart.	The Father shows an example of a glorified life through the son.

Another line of discipline or teaching is what the Father teaches us through the example of the life and role of the Son. We call this kind of wisdom Priestly Wisdom. Because of his love for his Father and his brothers, Jesus sacrificed himself on a cross as the Lamb of God. He made us blameless and spotless before the Father, once and for all, and qualified us as priests under himself. He is the Mediator of the New Covenant, where eternal life and the glory of God are promised and administered.

Examine the story of Solomon's wisdom with this perspective. It becomes quite illuminating. In 1 Kings 3, Solomon asked God for wisdom in order to rule His kingdom with justice and righteousness. God was so pleased at this request that He added all things to him. Jesus taught this same principle in Matthew 6:33, "But seek first his kingdom and his righteousness, and all these things will be given to you as well."

Before being given the kingdom, Solomon was brought up and trained in the courts of the House of God. He was under the guidance of the Levitical priesthood, who ministered before the Ark of the Lord, as well as in the court of the palace, under the guidance of his father and his officials under the rule of David as the king. During this time, the young man was entrusted with the task to build the Temple for the Lord, known as Solomon's Temple. This served as a type and shadow for the things to come. The substance or reality for us is in Christ (Colossians 2:17).

Solomon mentioned this often in Proverbs:

PROVERBS 3:1-12
¹ My son, do not forget my teaching,
but keep my commands in your heart,
² for they will prolong your life many years
and bring you prosperity.
³ Let love and faithfulness never leave you;

> *bind them around your neck,*
> *write them on the tablet of your heart.*
> *⁴ Then you will win favor and a good name*
> *in the sight of God and man.*
> *⁵ Trust in the Lord with all your heart*
> *and lean not on your own understanding;*
> *⁶ in all your ways acknowledge him,*
> *and he will make your paths straight.*
> *⁷ Do not be wise in your own eyes;*
> *fear the Lord and shun evil.*
> *⁸ This will bring health to your body*
> *and nourishment to your bones.*
> *⁹ Honor the Lord with your wealth,*
> *with the firstfruits of all your crops;*
> *¹⁰ then your barns will be filled to overflowing,*
> *and your vats will brim over with new wine.*
> *¹¹ My son, do not despise the Lord's discipline*
> *and do not resent his rebuke,*
> *¹² because the Lord disciplines those he loves,*
> *as a father the son he delights in.*

FATHER'S DISCIPLINE TO A SON

As mentioned before, God created man to be His son. His desire is to walk with man and discipline (disciple) him into His likeness, to be just like Him. Man was created to bear His name and to share His glory. This has always been the theme of His message to His chosen people.

Adam

Adam was created as a son of God. God placed him in the Garden of Eden and put him in charge over everything. He gave him the wisdom and understanding to name everything and rule everything. As his Father, God would walk with man and fellowship with him, teaching him everything until the day Adam fell.

From Abraham to the Israelites

God called Abraham out of the Chaldeans in Babylon, and promised him a land, and the hope that his descendants would become as numerous as the stars in the sky and many nations on earth (see Genesis 15).

In his old age, God blessed Abraham and Sarah with a son, Isaac. Isaac was gentle, godly, and obedient. In many ways, he foreshadowed the Lord Jesus Christ. However, Isaac was not good at disciplining his own twin sons. The firstborn, Esau, became a ruthless and violent man who indulged in hunting games and seldom paid attention to the things passed on to him from his forefathers. These were the very things in the heart of God. Later, for a bowl of soup, he was foolish enough to sell his birthright to his younger brother Jacob. Jacob was a "mother's boy" when he was young. He was quiet and ambitious, and very discontent with the fact that he was inferior to his brother, who was born only moments ahead of him from their mother's womb. This ambition, with encouragement from his mother, led him to cheat the blessing intended for Esau from his father Isaac.

The Seed

Jacob then fled at the threat of Esau and got married to Leah and Rachel in the land of his mother. Jacob too, failed to discipline his sons and they brought constant pain to him. Joseph, his favorite, was sold into slavery by his own brothers! Only Judah seemed to care about the loss and sorrow suffered by his father. Many years later, Joseph was able to be reunited with his family and the brothers reconciled with one another. He had been elevated to a position second only to Pharaoh in Egypt and was thus was able to provide refuge and shelter for his family in a time of famine.

After 400 years, Joseph was forgotten and the rulers of Egypt became uneasy with the great increase of the population of the Israelites in the land. They began to enslave the Israelites. It was at that time that Moses was born, only to be raised up in the court of Egypt as a prince. We know the story well. God ordained his path and he became a shepherd in an alien land only to be called back to Egypt and deliver his people out of the cruelty of slavery. After passing over the Red Sea, the Israelites wandered in the wilderness for 40 years. A generation passed away because they refused to yield to the discipline of God and provoked Him to anger—even Moses was excluded from going into the Promised Land. Facing their "homeland" on the other side of the Jordan, Moses declared the commands of God to a new generation of Israelites. He touched the essence of the law, the lesson that God intended to teach His people during these sorrowful yet meaningful 40 years.

DEUTERONOMY 8:1–5

[1] Be careful to follow every command I am giving you today, so that you may live and increase and may enter and possess the land that the Lord promised on oath to your forefathers. [2] Remember how the

Lord your God led you all the way in the desert these forty years, to humble you and to test you to know what was in your heart, whether you would keep his commands. ³ He humbled you, causing you to hunger and then feeding you with manna, which neither you nor your fathers had known, to teach you that man does not live on bread alone but on every word, that comes from the mouth of the Lord. ⁴ Your clothes did not wear out and your feet did not swell during these forty years. ⁵ Know then in your heart that as a man disciplines his son, so the Lord your God disciplines you.

From Jesus Christ to Us

It was never God's intention for His people to be bound by the law. Rather, He wanted to teach them His heart and His Goodness—embodied in the law. Until the Spirit was granted, a veil was over their minds so that they could not understand and gain wisdom (see 2 Corinthians 3).

The author of Hebrews explains this very well:

HEBREWS 12:1–11
¹ Therefore, since we are surrounded by such a great cloud of witnesses, let us throw off everything that hinders and the sin that so easily entangles, and let us run with perseverance the race marked out for us. ² Let us fix our eyes on Jesus, the author and perfecter of our faith, who for the joy set before him endured the cross, scorning its shame, and sat down at the right hand of the throne of God. ³ Consider him who endured such opposition from sinful men, so that you will not grow weary and lose heart.

⁴ In your struggle against sin, you have not yet resisted to the point of shedding your blood. ⁵ And you have forgotten that word of

> *encouragement that addresses you as sons:*
>
>> "*My son, do not make light of the Lord's discipline,*
>> *and do not lose heart when he rebukes you,*
>> *⁶ because the Lord disciplines those he loves,*
>> *and he punishes everyone he accepts as a son."*
>
> *⁷ Endure hardship as discipline; God is treating you as sons. For what son is not disciplined by his father? ⁸ If you are not disciplined (and everyone undergoes discipline), then you are illegitimate children and not true sons. ⁹ Moreover, we have all had human fathers who disciplined us and we respected them for it. How much more should we submit to the Father of our spirits and live!¹⁰ Our fathers disciplined us for a little while as they thought best; but God disciplines us for our good, that we may share in his holiness. ¹¹ No discipline seems pleasant at the time, but painful. Later, however, it produces a harvest of righteousness and peace for those who have been trained by it.*

SELF-DISCIPLINE AND DISCIPLINE WITHIN GOD'S FAMILY

Now, The Lord entrusts this discipline to us through three parties:

1. The Holy Spirit

2. God's Family, or the Body of Christ

3. One's Self

The Holy Spirit

Jesus shared with his disciples before he went to the cross that it's for their benefit that he should go, and another helper will be sent on his behalf to teach them.

JOHN 14:25-26

²⁵ "All this I have spoken while still with you. ²⁶ But the Counselor, the Holy Spirit, whom the Father will send in my name, will teach you all things and will remind you of everything I have said to you.

JOHN 16:7-8

⁷ But I tell you the truth: It is for your good that I am going away. Unless I go away, the Counselor will not come to you; but if I go, I will send him to you. ⁸ When he comes, he will convict the world of guilt in regard to sin and righteousness and judgment:

JOHN 16:12-16

¹² "I have much more to say to you, more than you can now bear. ¹³ But when he, the Spirit of truth, comes, he will guide you into all truth. He will not speak on his own; he will speak only what he hears, and he will tell you what is yet to come. ¹⁴ He will bring glory to me by taking from what is mine and making it known to you. ¹⁵ All that belongs to the Father is mine. That is why I said the Spirit will take from what is mine and make it known to you.

¹⁶ Jesus went on to say, "In a little while you will see me no more, and then after a little while you will see me."

God's Family, or the Body of Christ

Jesus commissioned Peter and the other apostles to disciple

others as he had discipled them. He also entrusted them with the duty and wisdom to bring the necessary discipline to those whom they would relate his teachings. God granted them the spiritual gifts, authority, and power to do so. These were given in order to impart God's wisdom and life to the members of the Body of Christ.

> **MATTHEW 10:24-25**
> *24 "A student is not above his teacher, nor a servant above his master. 25 It is enough for the student to be like his teacher, and the servant like his master. If the head of the house has been called Beelzebub, how much more the members of his household!*

> **EPHESIANS 4:11-16**
> *11 It was he who gave some to be apostles, some to be prophets, some to be evangelists, and some to be pastors and teachers, 12 to prepare God's people for works of service, so that the body of Christ may be built up 13 until we all reach unity in the faith and in the knowledge of the Son of God and become mature, attaining to the whole measure of the fullness of Christ.*
> *14 Then we will no longer be infants, tossed back and forth by the waves, and blown here and there by every wind of teaching and by the cunning and craftiness of men in their deceitful scheming.*
> *15 Instead, speaking the truth in love, we will in all things grow up into him who is the Head, that is, Christ. 16 From him the whole body, joined and held together by every supporting ligament, grows and builds itself up in love, as each part does its work.*

One's Self

It is imperative for us to know that though we are created by God and He orders our steps, we are still able to exercise our freewill. This means that we can choose to obey or to disobey God. It was God's intention that the Israelites would learn in their hearts to believe and trust Him. Yet they did not and thus provoked Him into anger. Consequently, a whole generation of them wandered in the wilderness for 40 years and died. Then God raised up another generation to continue the mission He had called them into.

God gives us the ability to exercise self-will, yet it pleases Him and glorifies Him when we choose to lay our will aside and yield to His will. This is the essence of the life of Jesus in human form. Facing every trial and temptation, he did not sin. He learned obedience through the things he suffered, even to the point of death on the cross.

HEBREWS 2:14–18

¹⁴ Since the children have flesh and blood, he too shared in their humanity so that by his death he might destroy him who holds the power of death—that is, the devil— ¹⁵ and free those who all their lives were held in slavery by their fear of death. ¹⁶ For surely it is not angels he helps, but Abraham's descendants. ¹⁷ For this reason he had to be made like his brothers in every way, in order that he might become a merciful and faithful high priest in service to God, and that he might make atonement for the sins of the people. ¹⁸ Because he himself suffered when he was tempted, he is able to help those who are being tempted.

> **"God gives us the ability to exercise self-will, yet it pleases Him and glorifies Him when we choose to lay our will aside and yield to His will."**

This is self-discipline. It has to do with the ability that God gave man to make the "right choices." Out of our love for Him, we would choose to obey Him, even when we might not understand everything that He commands us to do. This is the essence of the work of faith.

ROMANS 6:8–14

⁸ Now if we died with Christ, we believe that we will also live with him. ⁹ For we know that since Christ was raised from the dead, he cannot die again; death no longer has mastery over him. ¹⁰ The death he died, he died to sin once for all; but the life he lives, he lives to God.

¹¹ In the same way, count yourselves dead to sin but alive to God in Christ Jesus. ¹² Therefore do not let sin reign in your mortal body so that you obey its evil desires. ¹³ Do not offer the parts of your body to sin, as instruments of wickedness, but rather offer yourselves to God, as those who have been brought from death to life; and offer the parts of your body to him as instruments of righteousness. ¹⁴ For sin shall not be your master, because you are not under law, but under grace.

ROMANS 8:12–14

¹² Therefore, brothers, we have an obligation—but it is not to the sinful nature, to live according to it. ¹³ For if you live according to the sinful nature, you will die; but if by the Spirit you put to death the misdeeds of the body, you will live,
¹⁴ because those who are led by the Spirit of God are sons of God.

HOLINESS

The end or the final product of godly discipline is not that we become a showcase of how godly or spiritual we are, nor that we have become workers of miracles, signs, and wonders for God. Instead it is that we are truly able to abide in Him and "bear much fruit" as mentioned in chapter 6 of this book, "Spiritual Life" (see John 15:5).

In other words, we can live a life in and by the Spirit, which is life in the Kingdom of God.

> **ROMANS 14:17**
> *17 For the kingdom of God is not a matter of eating and drinking, but of righteousness, peace and joy in the Holy Spirit.*

This means that we have to consciously identify ourselves with the Lord and abide in Him, being set apart from this world. This is holiness.

> **JOHN 17:14–19**
> *14 I have given them your word and the world has hated them, for they are not of the world any more than I am of the world. 15 My prayer is not that you take them out of the world but that you protect them from the evil one. 16 They are not of the world, even as I am not of it. 17 Sanctify them by the truth; your word is truth. 18 As you sent me into the world, I have sent them into the world. 19 For them I sanctify myself, that they too may be truly sanctified.*

> **1 PETER 1:13–16**
> *13 Therefore, prepare your minds for action; be self-controlled; set your hope fully on the grace to be given you when Jesus Christ is revealed.*
> *14 As obedient children, do not conform to the evil desires you had when you lived in ignorance. 15 But just as he who called you is holy,*

so be holy in all you do; ^{16} *for it is written: "Be holy, because I am holy."*

> SCRIPTURES

Sanctification and Discipline

1 CORINTHIANS 6:9-11
⁹ Do you not know that the wicked will not inherit the kingdom of God? Do not be deceived: Neither the sexually immoral nor idolaters nor adulterers nor male prostitutes nor homosexual offenders ¹⁰ nor thieves nor the greedy nor drunkards nor slanderers nor swindlers will inherit the kingdom of God. ¹¹ And that is what some of you were. But you were washed, you were sanctified, you were justified in the name of the Lord Jesus Christ and by the Spirit of our God.

REVELATION 3:19
¹⁹ Those whom I love I rebuke and discipline. So be earnest, and repent.

1 CORINTHIANS 11:32
³² When we are judged by the Lord, we are being disciplined so that we will not be condemned with the world.

2 TIMOTHY 1:7
⁷ For God did not give us a spirit of timidity, but a spirit of power, of love and of self-discipline.

1 CORINTHIANS 9:24-27
²⁴ Do you not know that in a race all the runners run, but only one gets the prize? Run in such a way as to get the prize. ²⁵ Everyone who competes in the games goes into strict training. They do it to get a crown that will not last; but we do it to get a crown that will last forever. ²⁶ Therefore I do not run like a man running aimlessly; I do not fight like a man beating the air. ²⁷ No, I beat my body and make it my slave so that after I have preached to others; I myself will not be disqualified for the prize.

Holiness

2 CORINTHIANS 6:16–18

¹⁶ What agreement is there between the temple of God and idols? For we are the temple of the living God. As God has said: *"I will live with them and walk among them, and I will be their God, and they will be my people."*
¹⁷ *"Therefore come out from them and be separate, says the Lord. Touch no unclean thing, and I will receive you."*
¹⁸ *"I will be a Father to you, and you will be my sons and daughters, says the Lord Almighty."*

1 PETER 2:9

⁹ *But you are a chosen people, a royal priesthood, a holy nation, a people belonging to God, that you may declare the praises of him who called you out of darkness into his wonderful light.*

QUESTIONS FOR REVIEW

1. Consider the relationship between sanctification and discipline. Expound.

2. What are your thoughts about the relationship between discipleship and discipline?

3. What is the result of a relationship between a father and son when they interact with honor and love toward one another as the son grows up in the father's care?

4. How would you compare and contrast the discipline of the Father in heaven with self-discipline? How do they work together for us?

_____

_____

_____

5. What is holiness? Is holiness a state of being or a process of development?

_____

_____

_____

QUESTIONS
FOR MEDITATION & APPLICATION

1. How many disciplines have you engaged within your life? Review them in terms of your feeling towards them and the requirements and results of each.

_____

_____

_____

2. What is common in these disciplines? Do you think they are necessary? What makes you like or dislike certain ones?

_____

_____

_____

3. What do you think of the role of the Holy Spirit in your life as a son of God?

_____

_____

_____

_____

4. Is there any area you need to improve in terms of self-discipline, especially in your spiritual life?

_____

_____

_____

5. What does holiness mean to you in terms of your relationship to the world at this point in life?

_____

_____

_____

10

THE ORDER OF MELCHIZEDEK

OVERVIEW

In this chapter, we will survey the Order of Melchizedek:

- The Order of Melchizedek.

- A Survey of Types and Shadows

- Seven Covenants

- The Restoration after the Babylonian Exile

THE ORDER OF MELCHIZEDEK

In the book of Hebrews starting in chapter 7, the author begins to expound on the Order of Melchizedek, under which Jesus Christ has been established forever as the High Priest.

Who is Melchizedek?

Recorded in Genesis 14 is a certain person with the name Melchizedek, who was acting, at the time, as the king of Salem (later, Jerusalem) as well the as priest unto the Most High. He was obviously not a Hebrew according to the linage of Abraham. Now, it happened that Lot (Abram's nephew) was taken captive by the northern kings who tried to invade and plunder the Jordan valley. Abram came to his rescue. He won a great victory, restoring everything not only for his relative but also for the southern kings. Yet, even with such a great victory, he yielded humbly to be blessed under the governmental order that Melchizedek represented. Evidently in Abram's eyes, this order was much more than just a simple theocracy—which was common in those days.

Through this mystical encounter, Abram began to recognize that the God who had called him out of his homeland to a walk of faith was not just any god. Abram began to acknowledge Him as the Most High, the creator of heaven and earth. This holy deity from on high would not have Himself represented by any image or idol that is made through the imagination and efforts of man. But He had His living representation on earth in the person of a priest and king, Melchizedek. In whom he vested a priesthood of honor and glory and even the holiness of His Name.

This priesthood serves an even greater purpose than as only a mediator between God and man. It also claims sovereignty over all other kingdoms or peoples, whose right and life comes from God. Therefore, this position of a royal priesthood naturally has the right to claim tribute and support from they who are its subjects. In a sense, Abram's act of honor and worship should have served as a testimony to all the kingdoms or peoples around that his people or tribe will honor, support, and yield to the rule of the Most High. Interestingly, as the story tells it, among the kings who witnessed this act of worship were the kings of Sodom and Gamorra, whose kingdoms were judged by God with total destruction shortly after.

In their teachings, Jesus, Peter, and others later used this story as an example of the judgment reserved for our present, evil age, that is the judgment of fire. When the king of Sodom made a gesture of kindness to Abram by gifting him with his belongings, Abram rejected him. He would have no dealings with this wicked king. Abram also released the three Amorite brothers from their treaty of alliance. These resolute acts of allegiance serve as a divine principle for the people of God. We are to separate ourselves from this wicked world in order to be set apart unto God as His holy remnant, His called-out ones.

GENESIS 14:18–20

[18] Then Melchizedek king of Salem brought out bread and wine. He was priest of God Most High, [19] and he blessed Abram, saying, "Blessed be Abram by God Most High, Creator of heaven and earth. [20] And blessed be God Most High, who delivered your enemies into your hand."
Then Abram gave him a tenth of everything.

It was after this encounter that God visited Abram and promised to be his reward.

> **GENESIS 15:1–3**
>
> *¹ After this, the word of the Lord came to Abram in a vision: "Do not be afraid, Abram. I am your shield, your very great reward."*
> *² But Abram said, "O Sovereign Lord, what can you give me since I remain childless and the one who will inherit my estate is Eliezer of Damascus?" ³ And Abram said, "You have given me no children; so a servant in my household will be my heir."*

In response to Abram's request for an heir, God made a covenant with him. He put Abram into a deep sleep and made an "oath with Himself," promising not only an heir, but also the land which would come to be known as the Promised Land. This serves as a picture of the eternal covenant between God the Father and the Son for the benefit of man. As the beneficiary of this covenant, Abram was chosen by God to be the one through whom He would fulfill His eternal covenant for man.

The author of Hebrews explains it well:

> **HEBREWS 7:1–4**
>
> *¹ This Melchizedek was king of Salem and priest of God Most High. He met Abraham returning from the defeat of the kings and blessed him, ² and Abraham gave him a tenth of everything. First, his name means "king of righteousness"; then also, "king of Salem" means "king of peace." ³ Without father or mother, without genealogy, without beginning of days or end of life, like the Son of God he remains a priest forever.*

⁴ *Just think how great he was: Even the patriarch Abraham gave him a tenth of the plunder!*

Jesus as High Priest under the Order of Melchizedek

Jesus, like Melchizedek, belongs to a priesthood better than the Levitical priesthood, which was based on the law God gave to the Israelites through Moses.

In the latter part of Hebrews 7, the author explains another Old Testament prophecy by King David.

PSALM 110

¹ *The LORD says to my Lord:*
"Sit at my right hand
until I make your enemies
a footstool for your feet."
² *The LORD will extend your mighty scepter from Zion, saying,*
"Rule in the midst of your enemies!"
³ *Your troops will be willing*
on your day of battle.
Arrayed in holy splendor,
your young men will come to you
like dew from the morning's womb.
⁴ *The Lord has sworn*
and will not change his mind:
"You are a priest forever,
in the order of Melchizedek."
⁵ *The Lord is at your right hand;*
he will crush kings on the day of his wrath.
⁶ *He will judge the nations, heaping up the dead*

and crushing the rulers of the whole earth.
*⁷ He will drink from a brook beside the way;
therefore he will lift up his head.*

HEBREWS 7:15-25
*¹⁵ And what we have said is even more clear if another priest like Melchizedek appears, ¹⁶ one who has become a priest not on the basis of a regulation as to his ancestry but on the basis of the power of an indestructible life. ¹⁷ For it is declared:
"You are a priest forever, in the order of Melchizedek."
¹⁸ The former regulation is set aside because it was weak and useless ¹⁹ (for the law made nothing perfect), and a better hope is introduced, by which we draw near to God.
²⁰ And it was not without an oath! Others became priests without any oath, ²¹ but he became a priest with an oath when God said to him:
"The Lord has sworn and will not change his mind: 'You are a priest forever.'"
²² Because of this oath, Jesus has become the guarantee of a better covenant.
²³ Now there have been many of those priests, since death prevented them from continuing in office; ²⁴ but because Jesus lives forever, he has a permanent priesthood. ²⁵ Therefore he is able to save completely those who come to God through him, because he always lives to intercede for them.*

What is the Order of Melchizedek?

This priesthood is the eternal priesthood which functions in the heavenly tabernacle and is destined to come to earth through the Kingdom of Christ. Moses was given a vision of the pattern of this tabernacle in the angelic realm while on

Mount Sinai. God instructed him to build a copy (shadow) of it on earth. After it was erected, Moses anointed Aaron and his sons and they became the Levitical priesthood that ministered under the law that God gave to Moses.

When Jesus, the last Adam, was raised from the dead, he became the firstborn from the dead. He was glorified, having offered the perfect atonement for the sin of man, and disarmed the power of sin and death for all the descendants of the first Adam. Jesus opened the way for those who believe in his name to have access to the Father in Heaven through His priestly ministry, "the way." This eternal priesthood is not based on the law.

In the law, the two parties of the covenant were unequally yoked because man, in the flesh, could never be perfected by observing the law, so he could never fulfill his part of the deal. However, the eternal covenant from before time began is based on an oath that God made unto Himself. It exists in the eternal realm, and was revealed in the earthly realm with its promises of blessings in the covenants that God made with man through the ages. So, in a sense, this covenant is unequally yoked towards God the Father because He sealed it with the holiness of His name in order to accomplish His work towards man. This work is

> **"Jesus opened the way for those who believe in his name to have access to the Father in Heaven through His priestly ministry…"**

the perfection of man so that he is able to receive the benefits of this eternal covenant. As mentioned before, the Father made an oath with the Son and promised that He would produce a family of sons through "man." This work was disrupted when man was tempted by the evil one in the garden and excluded from eternal life. In order to preserve His eternal covenant toward man, God made this promise to Abraham: that he would have a seed or a son, who would restore man to Himself as His sons. This seed is Jesus the Christ, who is the life-giving spirit (see Galatians 3:15-29).

Paul explains this amazing gift of eternal life for those who believe in this way:

2 CORINTHIANS 1:20-22
[20] For no matter how many promises God has made, they are "Yes" in Christ. And so through him the "Amen" is spoken by us to the glory of God. [21] Now it is God who makes both us and you stand firm in Christ. He anointed us, [22] set his seal of ownership on us, and put his Spirit in our hearts as a deposit, guaranteeing what is to come.

Under this covenant, those who put their faith in Christ will be given the Spirit of sonship. It will then inscribe the law of God's life in their hearts. This is the new covenant that God will make with His people (see Jeremiah 31, 2 Corinthians 3).

The law, or the Old Covenant, was given and administered by angels. This is not the case with the New Covenant, which is given and ministered by the Spirit of God, the Father, and the Son. The Spirit of the Son, or the Spirit of sonship, gives us life as children of God. The Holy Spirit is then sent to disciple us on behalf of the Father and the Son. On behalf of the Son, the Holy Spirit will teach us about the Father and the Kingdom of the Son. On behalf of the Father, the Holy Spirit will teach us about the Son and the Household of the Father.

Under both covenants, the priesthood was extended through sonship, ensuring that he who stands in the place of the father is able to bear the image and likeness of his father. In this light, it was said of Jesus: "the Son is the radiance of God's glory and the exact representation of his being" (see Hebrews 1:3).

Under the eternal covenant, the kingly duty and office and the priestly duty and office are one. So, Jesus Christ is both the King of Righteousness and Peace and the High Priest of eternal life. This is the essence of the Order of Melchizedek.

A SURVEY OF TYPES AND SHADOWS

We do want to expound on the practical side of our life as a disciple of Christ, because it is the primary content of our education in the life of a son of God.

Before we do however, we will briefly survey some types and shadows of the order of this Heavenly Priesthood.

The Covenant with Adam

As shared in chapter 5 on sonship, man (Adam) was included in the eternal covenant between the Father and the Son. God created the world, and man, and rested on the seventh day. He set man in the Garden of Eden and provided him with everything he needed. Beyond that, He told Adam and Eve to multiply and subdue all things. To rule creation on behalf of the Father was a kingly position, bringing His righteousness to the heart and soul of all that He had created.

He also told Adam to take care of the Garden. This priestly position was to show the goodness and glory of God to creation. Adam was to intercede on their behalf, making peace between God and all that He had created—in heaven and on earth.

Adam fell from this position, losing the privilege to be taught by God, and to be a representation of Him to the rest of creation.

Covenant with Seth

Sadly, within the second generation of man, brother began to murder brother. Blood was shed within the family. When sin overtook Cain, he killed his younger brother Abel.

In order to preserve a seed without the stain of sin or the blood of the innocent, God separated Seth. The meaning of Seth's name is "compensation." God intended for him to replace the righteous Abel, who was able to make acceptable sacrifices before Him. Only at that time, "men began to call on the name of the LORD." Moreover, He intended that through Seth, the natural "seed" of the covenant of sonship could be carried on.

GENESIS 5:1-3
¹ This is the written account of Adam's line. When God created man, he made him in the likeness of God. ² He created them male

> *and female and blessed them. And when they were created, he called them "man."* ³ *When Adam had lived 130 years, he had a son in his own likeness, in his own image; and he named him Seth.*

Hidden here is the word "likeness." This word points to the original intent of God for man to be "just like Him" in the Spirit and as a spiritual being. When God created "man" in flesh and blood, male and female, He created them in His "image" with a promise and hope that they would be transformed into His likeness. Seth was born in the likeness of Adam (man). Through this "compensation," Seth was made as a prophetic hope for man to be fully restored in God.

In a sense, God continued the covenant with His Son through Seth without counting man's sins against him because of the blood shed by the righteous Abel, who was a shadow of Christ Jesus, the atoning sacrifice of his own life.

This was the priesthood before Noah.

Covenant with Noah

It would not be long before this priesthood was corrupted again.

> **GENESIS 6:1-3**
> ¹ *When men began to increase in number on the earth and daughters were born to them,* ² *the sons of God saw that the daughters of men were beautiful, and they married any of them they chose.* ³ *Then the LORD said, "My Spirit will not contend with man forever, for he is mortal; his days will be a hundred and twenty years."*

I tend to believe, although many may disagree, that the

"sons of God" mentioned here are in fact the priests of the Living God. Like the sons of Eli and the sons of Samuel, they degraded themselves in the service unto the Lord and brought disgrace to His name. As a result, God became very grieved with the condition of man.

> **GENESIS 6:5-7**
> *⁵ The LORD saw how great man's wickedness on the earth had become, and that every inclination of the thoughts of his heart was only evil all the time. ⁶ The LORD was grieved that he had made man on the earth, and his heart was filled with pain. ⁷ So the LORD said, "I will wipe mankind, whom I have created, from the face of the earth—men and animals, and creatures that move along the ground, and birds of the air—for I am grieved that I have made them."*

God brought the flood upon the whole earth, and along with the animals in the ark, only the righteous Noah and his family were saved. The ark is a symbol of God's presence and grace. After He transferred them to a new land, God established a covenant with Noah.

He first restored the things that were destroyed by the flood to mankind.

> **GENESIS 8:15-17**
> *¹⁵ Then God said to Noah, ¹⁶ "Come out of the ark, you and your wife and your sons and their wives. ¹⁷ Bring out every kind of living creature that is with you—the birds, the animals, and all the creatures that move along the ground—so they can multiply on the earth and be fruitful and increase in number upon it."*

The Seed

He then assured Noah that He would separate the fate of creation from the fate of man. They would no longer be subject to the judgment that is due man.

> **GENESIS 8:20-22**
> *[20] Then Noah built an altar to the LORD and, taking some of all the clean animals and clean birds, he sacrificed burnt offerings on it. [21] The LORD smelled the pleasing aroma and said in his heart: "Never again will I curse the ground because of man, even though every inclination of his heart is evil from childhood. And never again will I destroy all living creatures, as I have done.*
> *[22] "As long as the earth endures, seed time and harvest, cold and heat, summer and winter, day and night will never cease."*

In a sense, God made an oath with Himself that He would preserve man as a race, even though man had lost his position to subdue everything or to represent God to creation. Actually, God had to separate the creation from His dealings with mankind. Man's sin was taken into account, but no solution was offered.

> **GENESIS 9:1-17**
> *[1] Then God blessed Noah and his sons, saying to them, "Be fruitful and increase in number and fill the earth. [2] The fear and dread of you will fall upon all the beasts of the earth and all the birds of the air, upon every creature that moves along the ground, and upon all the fish of the sea; they are given into your hands. [3] Everything that lives and moves will be food for you. Just as I gave you the green plants, I now give you everything.*
> *[4] "But you must not eat meat that has its life blood still in it. [5] And for your lifeblood I will surely demand an accounting. I will demand an accounting from every animal. And from each man, too, I will*

demand an accounting for the life of his fellow man.
⁶ "Whoever sheds the blood of man, by man shall his blood be shed; for in the image of God has God made man.
⁷ As for you, be fruitful and increase in number; multiply on the earth and increase upon it."
⁸ Then God said to Noah and to his sons with him: ⁹ "I now establish my covenant with you and with your descendants after you ¹⁰ and with every living creature that was with you—the birds, the livestock and all the wild animals, all those that came out of the ark with you—every living creature on earth. ¹¹ I establish my covenant with you: Never again will all life be cut off by the waters of a flood; never again will there be a flood to destroy the earth."
¹² And God said, "This is the sign of the covenant I am making between me and you and every living creature with you, a covenant for all generations to come: ¹³ I have set my rainbow in the clouds, and it will be the sign of the covenant between me and the earth. ¹⁴ Whenever I bring clouds over the earth and the rainbow appears in the clouds, ¹⁵ I will remember my covenant between me and you and all living creatures of every kind. Never again will the waters become a flood to destroy all life. ¹⁶ Whenever the rainbow appears in the clouds, I will see it and remember the everlasting covenant between God and all living creatures of every kind on the earth."
¹⁷ So God said to Noah, "This is the sign of the covenant I have established between me and all life on the earth."

Covenant with Abraham

Noah had three sons, Ham, Shem, and Japheth. Ham uncovered his father's nakedness, forfeiting his birthright in God and invoking a curse upon his son, Canaan. The priesthood was extended through Shem. Abram was born from the line of Shem. It is interesting to know that in later days, God led the Israelites out of Egypt to possess the land He had promised to Abraham, which was occupied by Canaanites at the time.

Now let's concentrate on the part concerning the covenant.

After God called Abram out of the Chaldeans and promised that He would bless him, Abram was 75 years old. He and his nephew Lot went separate ways. Lot was later looted by kings from the north and Abram came to his rescue. This is the story we looked at in the beginning of this chapter. He met Melchizedek and was blessed by Him.

Only after this did God establish a covenant with Abram (see Genesis 15). He promised him a son to be the heir of all the things that he would bless him with. However, many years passed, and Sarai was proven to be desolate or barren. Abram was already 99 years old, and their hope of bearing a son was totally sapped. So, God visited Abram again and conferred to him the covenant with the promise of a son as his heir. It was at this time that He changed Abram's name to Abraham. Later, after the covenant of circumcision, he also changed Sarai's name to Sarah. You may be familiar with the meaning and significance of Abram's name change, but what about Sarai's name? Sarai means "princess," Sarah means "honored woman" (mother with an heir). In those days, child bearing was so important for a wife that all her honor and hope hung on it. Sarah's new name meant that she was not only the precious love and wife of her husband, but that her shame of being barren was over and she would be honored as a mother through her son. In this light, we are to understand that, in these days the Church (as far as God is concerned) is breaking out of the desolation and barrenness of "the Church Age." She will finally be able to bear sons! These sons of God are being entrusted with the Order of Melchizedek and are able to now sow the genuine "seed of the Kingdom" into the hearts of men. God is restoring our desolate land. What was prophesied and cried for by Isaiah is coming to pass (see Isaiah 49:14–26; 54; 62:1–5; 66:7–13).

After a year had passed, Sarah gave birth to Isaac. Commanded by God, Abraham expelled Hagar and her son Ishmael because they caused constant trouble in the family.

When Isaac had grown older, God tested Abraham by asking him to sacrifice his son. Abraham obeyed. Because Isaac is a type or shadow of Jesus Christ here, the following provision from God demonstrates that He would be faithful to more than His personal commitment to Abraham, but also to His own Son.

GALATIANS 3:15-19 NASB

[15] Brethren, I speak in terms of human relations: even though it is only a man's covenant, yet when it has been ratified, no one sets it aside or adds conditions to it. [16] Now the promises were spoken to Abraham and to his seed. He does not say, "And to seeds," as referring to many, but rather to one, "And to your seed," that is, Christ. [17] What I am saying is this: the Law, which came four hundred and thirty years later, does not invalidate a covenant previously ratified by God, so as to nullify the promise. [18] For if the inheritance is based on law, it is no longer based on a promise; but God has granted it to Abraham by means of a promise.
[19] Why the Law then? It was added because of transgressions, having been ordained through angels by the agency of a mediator,

until the seed would come to whom the promise had been made.

Through faith, Abraham reactivated the "seed of promise" that had long been dead within mankind.

> **GENESIS 22:15-18**
> *[15] The angel of the LORD called to Abraham from heaven a second time [16] and said, "I swear by myself, declares the LORD, that because you have done this and have not withheld your son, your only son, [17] I will surely bless you and make your descendants as numerous as the stars in the sky and as the sand on the seashore. Your descendants will take possession of the cities of their enemies, [18] and through your offspring all nations on earth will be blessed, because you have obeyed me."*

The apostle Paul mentions the significance of this covenant:

> **ROMANS 4:18-25**
> *[18] Against all hope, Abraham in hope believed and so became the father of many nations, just as it had been said to him, "So shall your offspring be." [19] Without weakening in his faith, he faced the fact that his body was as good as dead—since he was about a hundred years old—and that Sarah's womb was also dead. [20] Yet he did not waver through unbelief regarding the promise of God, but was strengthened in his faith and gave glory to God, [21] being fully persuaded that God had power to do what he had promised. [22] This is why "it was credited to him as righteousness." [23] The words "it was credited to him" were written not for him alone, [24] but also for us, to whom God will credit righteousness—for us who believe in him who raised Jesus our Lord from the dead. [25] He was delivered over to death for our sins and was raised to life for our justification.*

Covenant with Jacob

In the last chapter, we mentioned how Jacob cheated the birthright as well as the blessings from his twin brother Esau. This invoked great anger from Esau, so much so that he wanted to kill Jacob.

Jacob had to flee from home. On his way to his uncle, God revealed Himself to Jacob and made a covenant with Him.

> **GENESIS 28:10–15**
> *[10] Jacob left Beersheba and set out for Haran. [11] When he reached a certain place, he stopped for the night because the sun had set. Taking one of the stones there, he put it under his head and lay down to sleep. [12] He had a dream in which he saw a stairway resting on the earth, with its top reaching to heaven, and the angels of God were ascending and descending on it. [13] There above it stood the LORD, and he said: "I am the LORD, the God of your father Abraham and the God of Isaac. I will give you and your descendants the land on which you are lying. [14] Your descendants will be like the dust of the earth, and you will spread out to the west and to the east, to the north and to the south. All peoples on earth will be blessed through you and your offspring. [15] I am with you and will watch over you wherever you go, and I will bring you back to this land. I will not leave you until I have done what I have promised you."*

There are at least three major differences between this covenant and the one that God made with his fathers:

1. His descendants would not be confined to the boundaries of the promised land. Instead, this promise would go out

in four directions to the ends of the earth.

2. It foretold a process of scattering and in-gathering.

3. This promise was given to not just an individual family, but to a people or a nation.

Later, God called Jacob to return to Bethel where he had had the dream. The night before he met Esau, he wrestled with God and prevailed, and God gave him a new name, Israel, which means "prince of God."

From Israel's 12 sons, the family grew to seventy in number before they came into Egypt to seek shelter and refuge from Joseph.

During the following 400 years, the Israelites increased greatly in number, amounting to millions in the time of Moses.

Covenant with Moses (The Israelites)

In Genesis 15, God foretold Abram that his descendants would suffer as aliens in a foreign land for 400 years.

According to Paul, it happened 430 years later, as the Israelites were enslaved by the Egyptians. God raised up Moses to lead them out of Egypt to the land that He had promised to their forefathers.

This is a familiar story so we will bypass it to get to the place when God gave the Old Covenant to the Israelites at Sinai.

EXODUS 19:3-6

³ Then Moses went up to God, and the LORD called to him from the mountain and said, "This is what you are to say to the house of Jacob and what you are to tell the people of Israel: ⁴ 'You yourselves have seen what I did to Egypt, and how I carried you on eagles' wings and brought you to myself. ⁵ Now if you obey me fully and keep my covenant, then out of all nations you will be my treasured possession. Although the whole earth is mine, ⁶ you will be for me a kingdom of priests and a holy nation.' These are the words you are to speak to the Israelites."

We can clearly see that God's intention was not to give the Israelites a law that they could never fulfill. Rather, He intended for them to be the fulfillment of His promise, so that they would be raised up as His holy people, a nation of priests unto other nations. Through them, He would teach other peoples and show them His glory and power, love and mercy, righteousness and justice.

Although God had preserved them, prepared them, delivered them, and guided them up to this point, His desire was never merely to give the Israelites the land that He had promised to their forefathers. Rather, He would have them be set apart for His own purposes, to bring salvation to all peoples, and thereby to restore His original intent for man.

He would be the King of a kingdom of priests, which means that they are all sons to Him. In the same context, we know that He had delivered the Israelites from slavery and had redeemed them from the judgment of death. God called them His "firstborn," implying a further blessed identity that He would have them assume—to rule or reign with Him in His

Kingdom. He would teach them more than Priestly wisdom, but also a Kingly wisdom. He would exalt them before the kings and princes of the earth. For in His eyes, Israel is His prince.

However, the Israelites fell into the sin unbelief and rebellion. They practiced rivalry and idolatry when Moses was summoned to the peak of Sinai to receive the law. Their hearts were dull of hearing. The wonderful promise of God was too much for them to understand and receive.

God, out of His love, and because of the mediation of Moses (who served as a type for Christ Jesus), lowered the standard and gave them the law. He did this in order to preserve the seed of His promise, not only to Abraham and Jacob, but also to His Son, the Christ.

Even so, God did not stop the work of the further revelation of what He intended for man through His eternal covenant with His Son. He would reveal His desire to have man as His royal sons (His Family), or princes in His Kingdom, by raising up a man after His own heart, David.

Covenant with David

When Moses' generation failed to obey God, they were left to die in the wilderness. God instructed Moses to establish Joshua and Caleb to succeed him to lead a new generation who would possess the Promised Land, which they did, and the age of judges began.

This age lasted over 400 years from the time of Joshua to the time of Samuel. Then the people began to desire a king to rule over them like the nations around them. God (through Samuel) gave them the king of their choice. Saul, a Benjamite, was selected and anointed to be the king for them. Later Saul, out of his rebellion and selfish desires, disqualified himself. God again had Samuel anoint David, who was only a shepherd boy at the time, and was ignored and despised even by his own family.

David was raised up by God to become more than a good shepherd, but also a great warrior, and a wonderful worshiper (with his harp and songs). This ensured his success in Saul's court and army, which ultimately provoked Saul to jealousy. In the end, David had to flee from his persecution, and hid in caves while wandering in the land of the Philistines. Through these trials, he grew in strength as a warrior, in royal and noble character as a leader, and in wisdom and godliness as a man with a heart after God.

Years came to pass and Saul and his son Jonathan died together in battle against the Philistines. This made way for David to be established as the king of God's people. The first seven and half years He was king over Judah, and then of all of Israel. He took back the city of Jerusalem. David then fortified Zion, and it was called the city of David. Now God had subdued all the surrounding kingdoms to David and He even used a foreign king to build him a palace.

David recovered the Ark from the Philistines, brought it back to Jerusalem, and pitched a tent for it. On the way, he dressed in a linen ephod, rejoicing and dancing. In this prophetic scene, David fulfilled two offices in one person: the kingly and the priestly.

However, he felt very unsettled that he himself was living in a palace that he did not build, while the Ark of the Lord remained in a shabby tent (Psalm 132). So, he set his heart to build God a "palace." Through the prophet Nathan, the LORD told him that he would not be the one who would build Him a house.

2 SAMUEL 7:12–16
[12] When your days are over and you rest with your fathers, I will raise up your offspring to succeed you, who will come from your own body, and I will establish his kingdom. [13] He is the one who will build a house for my Name, and I will establish the throne of his kingdom forever. [14] I will be his father, and he will be my son. When he does wrong, I will punish him with the rod of men, with floggings inflicted by men. [15] But my love will never be taken away from him, as I took it away from Saul, whom I removed from before you. [16] Your house and your kingdom will endure forever before me; your throne will be established forever.'"

We know it wasn't Solomon to who this referred, but Christ Jesus.

PSALM 89:19–29
[19] Once you spoke in a vision,
to your faithful people you said:
"I have bestowed strength on a warrior;
I have exalted a young man from among the people.
[20] I have found David my servant;
with my sacred oil I have anointed him.
[21] My hand will sustain him;

surely my arm will strengthen him.
²² No enemy will subject him to tribute;
no wicked man will oppress him.
²³ I will crush his foes before him
and strike down his adversaries.
²⁴ My faithful love will be with him,
and through my name his horn will be exalted.
²⁵ I will set his hand over the sea,
his right hand over the rivers.
²⁶ He will call out to me, 'You are my Father,
my God, the Rock my Savior.'
²⁷ I will also appoint him my firstborn,
the most exalted of the kings of the earth.
²⁸ I will maintain my love to him forever,
and my covenant with him will never fail.
²⁹ I will establish his line forever,
his throne as long as the heavens endure.

Building of the Second Temple

Before, in, and after the Babylonian Exile, God sent many prophets to the Israelites. They were sent to warn, rebuke, counsel, guide, comfort, and encourage His people. Some were badly mistreated and suffered a great deal even in the hands of their own people, like Isaiah and Jeremiah.

For 70 years, the Israelites could not get back to their homeland. Slowly, the younger generation became accustomed to the cultures in which they lived. The worship of false gods and intermarriage began to steal away the purity of their religion and tradition. God sent many prophets in the midst of them to encourage them to keep themselves as His remnant, setting

THE SEED

themselves apart as God's people. He warned them not to conform to the cultures around them. Finally, God began to miraculously restore his people. Leaders and groups of people began to come back to their homeland and a work to rebuild the temple and the city began. Joshua the high priest (of the line of Zadok) and Zerubbabel the governor (of the line of David) were given charge. Even so, according to prophetic words, they and their work were only a type and shadow of what was to come (see Zechariah 3:8).

The temple they built was to foreshadow the spiritual temple that God would build in the hearts of His people through Christ Jesus. Let's take a look:

HAGGAI 2:6-9
⁶ "This is what the LORD Almighty says: 'In a little while I will once more shake the heavens and the earth, the sea and the dry land. ⁷ I will shake all nations, and the desired of all nations will come, and I will fill this house with glory,' says the LORD Almighty. ⁸ 'The silver is mine and the gold is mine,' declares the LORD Almighty. ⁹ 'The glory of this present house will be greater than the glory of the former house,' says the LORD Almighty. 'And in this place I will grant peace,' declares the LORD Almighty."

In addition, there is a hidden work that God is orchestrating for the revelation of the Order of Melchizedek.

ZECHARIAH 6:11-13
¹¹ Take the silver and gold and make a crown, and set it on the head of the high priest, Joshua son of Jehozadak. ¹² Tell him this is what the LORD Almighty says: 'Here is the man whose name is the Branch, and he will branch out from his place and build the

temple of the LORD. *[13] It is he who will build the temple of the LORD, and he will be clothed with majesty and will sit and rule on his throne. And he will be a priest on his throne. And there will be harmony between the two.'*

In numerous prophecies, the Messiah is called "the branch." The prophetic meaning of the above scripture is that the office of kingship and the office of high priesthood will be one in Christ Jesus. Only under this order and oneness are ministers of the New Covenant established, first in the heavenly tabernacle, and then "on earth as it is in heaven."

SCRIPTURES

The Order of Melchizedek

1 PETER 1:9-10
⁹ for you are receiving the goal of your faith, the salvation of your souls. ¹⁰ Concerning this salvation, the prophets, who spoke of the grace that was to come to you, searched intently and with the greatest care,

REVELATION 1:5-6
⁵ and from Jesus Christ, who is the faithful witness, the firstborn from the dead, and the ruler of the kings of the earth. To him who loves us and has freed us from our sins by his blood, ⁶ and has made us to be a kingdom and priests to serve his God and Father—to him be glory and power for ever and ever! Amen.

Types and Shadows

GENESIS 1:27-28
²⁷ So God created man in his own image, in the image of God he created him; male and female he created them. ²⁸ God blessed them and said to them, "Be fruitful and increase in number; fill the earth and subdue it. Rule over the fish of the sea and the birds of the air and over every living creature that moves on the ground."

GENESIS 4:25-26; 5:1-3
²⁵ Adam lay with his wife again, and she gave birth to a son and named him Seth, saying, "God has granted me another child in place of Abel, since Cain killed him." ²⁶ Seth also had a son, and he named him Enosh. At that time men began to call on the name of the LORD.

¹ This is the written account of Adam's line. When God created man, he made him in the likeness of God. ² He created them male and female and blessed them. And when they were created, he called them "man." ³ When Adam had lived 130 years, he had a son in his own likeness, in his own image; and he named him Seth.

GENESIS 6:17–18

¹⁷ I am going to bring floodwaters on the earth to destroy all life under the heavens, every creature that has the breath of life in it. Everything on earth will perish. ¹⁸ But I will establish my covenant with you, and you will enter the ark—you and your sons and your wife and your sons' wives with you.

GENESIS 17:3–8

³ Abram fell facedown, and God said to him, ⁴ "As for me, this is my covenant with you: You will be the father of many nations. ⁵ No longer will you be called Abram; your name will be Abraham, for I have made you a father of many nations. ⁶ I will make you very fruitful; I will make nations of you, and kings will come from you. ⁷ I will establish my covenant as an everlasting covenant between me and you and your descendants after you for the generations to come, to be your God and the God of your descendants after you. ⁸ The whole land of Canaan, where you are now an alien, I will give as an everlasting possession to you and your descendants after you; and I will be their God."

GENESIS 35:11–15

¹¹ And God said to him, "I am God Almighty; be fruitful and increase in number. A nation and a community of nations will come from you, and kings will come from your body. ¹² The land I gave to Abraham and Isaac I also give to you, and I will give this land to your descendants after you."
¹³ Then God went up from him at the place where he had talked with him. ¹⁴ Jacob set up a stone pillar at the place where God had talked

with him, and he poured out a drink offering on it; he also poured oil on it. ⁱ⁵ Jacob called the place where God had talked with him Bethel.

EXODUS 34:27–28

²⁷ Then the LORD said to Moses, "Write down these words, for in accordance with these words I have made a covenant with you and with Israel." ²⁸ Moses was there with the LORD forty days and forty nights without eating bread or drinking water. And he wrote on the tablets the words of the covenant—the Ten Commandments.

QUESTIONS FOR REVIEW

1. In Hebrew, the name "Melchizedek" means king of "righteousness." Salem, his kingdom means, "peace." What is your understanding of this in the context of the Kingdom of God?

_____

_____

_____

2. After you read the types and shadows of the Order of Melchizedek, please read 2 Corinthians 3. How do you compare the ministry under the law with that of the Spirit?

_____

_____

_____

QUESTIONS
FOR MEDITATION & APPLICATION

1. Read Hebrews chapters 7 and 8. Where do you think Jesus Christ is acting as the High Priest? Please explain.

_____

_____

_____

2. When you have just been born again, do you think you are immediately qualified to be a minister of the New Covenant? Why?

_____

_____

_____

3. Do you think there is a difference between spiritual life and spiritual ministry? Please explain.

_____

_____

11

MINISTRY OF THE NEW COVENANT

OVERVIEW

In this chapter, we will discuss the ministry of the New Covenant in the light of kingly and priestly offices:

- Ministry of the New Covenant

- Key Observations of the Kingly and Priestly Office and Duty

In the last chapter, we touched on the Order of Melchizedek. We are to minister under this order after we are established in the Household of God the Father, and in the Kingdom of Christ as a son of God. In this chapter, we will continue with this discussion.

In the past 2000 years, the followers of Christ have made many attempts to restore the practices of the early church, earnestly seeking to recover its past glory. Some have succeeded to a certain extent, and others were just the efforts of men charged with religious zeal. Upon closer inspection, it seems that these attempts always intended to create an antidote for the ills of the day: the apathy of believers, the corruption of church, the decadence of society, and the decline of culture.

For these zealous souls, the norm of the day could no longer constrain their passion and expectation. In response to their dissatisfaction and disillusionment, the Lord would answer their cry for reformation or revival. Through them, He would bring a measure of improvement to the people and the culture of the day.

Yet even the best of these "movements" seem to never go beyond the framework of a "past glory." Each one has gradually receded as the purity and the spirit of the early church began to dwindle. As a result, any effort to "institutionalize" what had been achieved, has served as a clear sign that a movement or revival has begun to wane. Able men and women, concerned about their cause, would formulate and emphasize their way of doing things, stipulated by their brand of biblical or spiritual understandings and convictions. This is especially true for modern day Christianity, evidenced by the explosion

> "It is our hope that these writings will somehow enable you to depart from the 'Egypt' of this world, and the 'Babylon' of false religion, and to worship the Most High God in the New Jerusalem of Heaven. Not in the future, but 'here and now,' 'in spirit and in truth.'"

of many denominations and the springing up of various movements in recent history.

Is this the norm? Should this be the norm? Will this be the norm? The answer to each is a resounding NO.

A people who are being prepared, even now, to be endowed with the Lord's wisdom and grace will yet again unveil God's plan for His people. They will lead us back to the "ancient path" carved out by the "ancient of days." This is not wishy-washy thinking on any man's part. No, this is precisely what is repeatedly prophesied in the Old Testament (Psalm 24:6; Psalm 110; Daniel 12:1–4; Isaiah 66:18–24; Haggai 2:6–9; Malachi 4), as well as in the New Testament (Matthew 13:39–43; Matthew 24–25).

For the above prophecies to come to pass, a restoration of the foundation of what has long been "lost" concerning the teachings of Jesus Christ will be inevitable. That is, genuine discipleship in the context of a life in the Kingdom of God by the Spirit, not in the context of a life built upon man's traditions. It is our hope that these writings will somehow enable you to depart from the "Egypt" of this world, and the "Babylon" of false religion, and to worship the Most High God in the New Jerusalem of Heaven. Not in the future, but "here and now," "in spirit and in truth."

Teachings of this nature will bear certain characteristics. Here are a few:

1. They will not be founded upon the traditions and rules of man; nor will they end there. Rather, they will be oriented in the Kingdom of God and centered around one's spiritual life—the new life in Christ Jesus.

2. They will not appeal to or be fulfilled by man's intellect, but by the power of the Holy Spirit—the spirit of wisdom and understanding, as the apostle Paul put it.

3. They are not to reform or perfect a movement or a religious system, but are to release and establish us into eternal life with the Kingdom Reality.

4. They will be the real return to the New Covenant ministry, with the same authority and power granted to the disciples when the Lord sent them out to disciple the nations (peoples) (see Matthew 28).

THE NEW COVENANT MINISTRY

Promised in the Old Testament

JEREMIAH 31:31-34

³¹ "The days are coming," declares the Lord, "when I will make a new covenant with the people of Israel and with the people of Judah. ³² It will not be like the covenant I made with their ancestors when I took them by the hand to lead them out of Egypt, because they broke my covenant, though I was a husband to them," declares the Lord. ³³ "This is the covenant I will make with the people of Israel after that time," declares the Lord. "I will put my law in their minds and write it on their hearts. I will be their God, and they will be my people. ³⁴ No longer will they teach their neighbor, or say to one another, 'Know the Lord,' because they will all know me, from the least of them to the greatest," declares the Lord. "For I will forgive their wickedness and will remember their sins no more."

EZEKIEL 37:26-27

²⁶ I will make a covenant of peace with them; it will be an everlasting covenant. I will establish them and increase their numbers, and I will put my sanctuary among them forever. ²⁷ My dwelling place will be with them; I will be their God, and they will be my people.

Fulfilled by Jesus

These prophecies were fulfilled when Jesus Christ, who is from the line of David in the flesh, chose to die on the cross as the Son of God and the Son of Man. He nullified the law of sin and death once and for all, and established the covenant of eternal life. The moment He died on the cross He exclaimed,

"It is finished." Indeed!

Entrusted to the Disciples

Before Jesus went to the cross, he had the Passover dinner with them. This is a symbolic act through which he instructed them to partake of his body and his blood. This set them apart as ministers of this New Covenant (see 1 Corinthians 11:23-26).

After he was resurrected, he came to his disciples and taught them for 40 days, and then instructed them to preach the gospel and to disciple all nations. But before that, he told them to tarry in Jerusalem until they received power from on High (see Matthew 28:16-20, Luke 24:45-53).

Then, on the day of Pentecost, they were baptized by the Holy Spirit and began to preach and share the gospel with conviction and power (see Acts 2-3).

Passed on to Us

This gospel was passed on to us as disciples of Jesus Christ. When Jesus prayed for the disciples before his Father, he included us in his prayer. Some refer to this as the High Priestly Prayer.

> **JOHN 17:20-22**
>
> [20] *"My prayer is not for them [the disciples] alone. I pray also for those who will believe in me through their message, [21] that all of them may be one, Father, just as you are in me and I am in you. May they also be in us so that the world may believe that you have sent me. [22] I have given them the glory that you gave me, that they*

may be one as we are one—"

Now, this oneness that Jesus prayed for is an inclusion of us as his Body, with himself being the Head. Certainly, this can't be a work done by man with his own strength and power, but only by the chosen vessels (the elected) that God raises up and empowers through the Holy Spirit.

This is the pattern or model of the ministry of the New Covenant, that through discipleship, we can learn His ways and receive the power of the Holy Spirit. After being firmly established in Him, we can then proceed to be about the Father's business as well.

This ministry is fundamentally different from the one under the Old Covenant. It is a ministry of God's eternal life and glory in the Spirit. It can't be accomplished, or even comprehended by man's flesh (see 2 Corinthians 3).

The Role of Both King and Priest

As we mentioned before, the role of the kingly office and duty is of discipline or discipleship in the Kingdom of God, whose king is the Lord Jesus Christ. The role of the priestly office and duty is of discipline or discipleship in the Family of God under the headship of Jesus Christ, who acts as the High Priest under the eternal covenant in the Heavenly Tabernacle. These are two inseparable realities that we will enter into after we are born again in Christ Jesus.

KEY OBSERVATIONS ON THE KINGLY AND PRIESTLY OFFICES AND DUTIES

The Kingdom of God is an invisible spiritual reality, flowing from and into an eternal reality. It is revealed through the Son of God, Jesus Christ, and is entrusted to Him. The perfection of such a reality can only be wrought through the divine order that is revealed through His ministry or discipleship, for life and peace (Malachi 2:4-6). When it is revealed through the Son, it is also perfect in every way pertaining to its order and function. Accordingly, we will be introduced to a reality of oneness, or fellowship—of <u>communion</u> with the Father and the Son, through the Holy Spirit, as we are perfected in Christ—in His life and in His ministry. Even more importantly, we will also <u>be transformed</u> from glory to glory in the life of God our Father. This transformation will be even until to fullness of the life of Christ Jesus, who is the exact representation and the perfect image of His Father.

In the very beginning, Christ (the Anointed one, the firstborn over all creation, through whom everything exists) chose to obey the Father because of his love for the Father. He identified with the Father's love toward His creation, the crown of which is man. At the appointed time, he was sent by the Father into the visible world, became a man of flesh (the last Adam), born of a woman, and endured all temptations and sufferings even unto death on a cross. Yet He was without sin and disobedience. Thus, he was perfect in every way as a son of man, and was able to embody the fullness of God's life as the Son of God to carry out the power of the Holy Spirit as the Anointed one. More than this, he who was without sin chose to be identified with sin, and was condemned to death, even to bear the wrath of God in its fullness. Therefore, he was able to disarm the power and dominion of sin and death and break off the bondage that the evil one had laid upon mankind. He offered himself as the perfect sacrifice once and for all. Having taken away the curse of sin and death, he sat down at the right hand of God and was given all authority and power over the evil one and his dominion, even for the benefit of those who believe in him.

Through our faith in Christ Jesus, we are then included in the Kingdom of Christ, having been delivered from the Kingdom of Darkness.

> **COLOSSIANS 1:13–14**
> *[13] For he has rescued us from the dominion of darkness and brought us into the kingdom of the Son he loves, [14] in whom we have redemption, the forgiveness of sins.*

However, this Kingdom is not isolated from God's Family; rather it is one with the Family of our heavenly Father. Let's offer some observations on this.

The intent of God the Father was never just to be acknowledged as the Creator (Jehovah, Genesis 14:22), or just to be exalted as the Most High (El Elyon), or just to be worshiped as the Almighty (El Shaddai, Genesis 17:1). That is, He does not want to merely be worshiped as God. Rather, it was and is His desire to have man included as His Family. That through man, He would subdue all creation and make His name known to them. That is, He wants to reveal His fatherhood to man and through man, unto all creation. God the Father is love and Christ Jesus is the perfect expression of that love, even through His sonship. Yes, God is the Sovereign One (Jehovah or Creator) and Lord over all that He created. Yet, before He created anything, He set apart man to be His own representation, His embodiment, to govern and administrate His perfect will concerning all that which is created. Thereby His love and wisdom, His righteousness and justice, His faithfulness and goodness can be made known unto all creation (1 Timothy 3:15–4:9, Colossians 1:9–29).

When we are saved through Christ Jesus, we are restored to this inheritance in God the Father as His children. We become co-heirs with Christ Jesus in His Family, and we are to rule creation with him. In this we derive our kingly office and duty in Christ.

> **ROMANS 8:17**
> *17 Now if we are children, then we are heirs—heirs of God and co-heirs with Christ, if indeed we share in his sufferings in order that we may also share in his glory.*

> **ROMANS 8:29–30**
> *29 For those God foreknew he also predestined to be conformed to the likeness of his Son, that he might be the firstborn among many brothers. 30 And those he predestined, he also called; those he called, he also justified; those he justified, he also glorified.*

In order to be empowered and transformed to be able to rule creation with Him, this scripture reveals God's process with us. First, He adopts us as His sons through Christ Jesus. This adoption grafts us into His Family, His Household. Here we have been predestined and called. Second, He will teach us kingly and priestly wisdom. These two kinds of wisdom (as we mentioned before) are taught through the Holy Spirit, as His royal sons. Within this second process we are sanctified and justified. Third, when we are established in His wisdom, He will give us the authority and the power to go about His business. This empowerment is where we are glorified and sent.

1. Adoption (Predestination and calling)

2. Teaching of Kingly and Priestly wisdom (Sanctification and justification)

3. Giving of Authority and Power (Glorification and sending out)

Our Lord Jesus demonstrated this pattern of life and growth. Our life in God the Father is indeed one that grows from grace to grace (empowerment), and from glory to glory (transformation).

As God's chosen people, we are to be a kingdom of God's priests, making His name known to all creation. When God created man, this was the true and ultimate intention of His heart. When he called and set apart the Israelites as a people, when He gave His son, when He renewed His promises with His people, "the knowledge of the glory of the LORD" (Isaiah 11:9, Habakkuk 2:14) to be made known through His royal sons flows as the undercurrent through it all.

1 PETER 2:9

⁹ But you are a chosen people, a royal priesthood, a holy nation, a people belonging to God, that you may declare the praises of him who called you out of darkness into his wonderful light.

REVELATION 1:6

⁶ and has made us to be a kingdom and priests to serve his God and Father—to him be glory and power for ever and ever! Amen.

Notice that the way of rule or reign in the Kingdom of God is not like the way of the world, which is ruled by the evil one, rather it is the opposite. Jesus explains this very well:

LUKE 22:25-30

²⁵ Jesus said to them, "The kings of the Gentiles lord it over them; and those who exercise authority over them call themselves Benefactors. ²⁶ But you are not to be like that. Instead, the greatest among you should be like the youngest, and the one who rules like the one who serves. ²⁷ For who is greater, the one who is at the table or the one who serves? Is it not the one who is at the table? But I am among you as one who serves. ²⁸ You are those who have stood by me in my trials. ²⁹ And I confer on you a kingdom, just as my Father conferred one on me, ³⁰ so that you may eat and drink at my table in my kingdom and sit on thrones, judging the twelve tribes of Israel.

The authority and power conferred to us in the Kingdom of God is given to help others come to know Him and to be built up in Him. In essence, this is our priestly office and duty.

SCRIPTURES

The New Covenant Ministry

2 CORINTHIANS 2:4-11

⁴ For I wrote you out of great distress and anguish of heart and with many tears, not to grieve you but to let you know the depth of my love for you.

⁵ If anyone has caused grief, he has not so much grieved me as he has grieved all of you, to some extent—not to put it too severely. ⁶ The punishment inflicted on him by the majority is sufficient for him. ⁷ Now instead, you ought to forgive and comfort him, so that he will not be overwhelmed by excessive sorrow. ⁸ I urge you, therefore, to reaffirm your love for him. ⁹ The reason I wrote you was to see if you would stand the test and be obedient in everything. ¹⁰ If you forgive anyone, I also forgive him. And what I have forgiven—if there was anything to forgive—I have forgiven in the sight of Christ for your sake, ¹¹ in order that Satan might not outwit us. For we are not unaware of his schemes.

2 CORINTHIANS 5:18-19

¹⁸ All this is from God, who reconciled us to himself through Christ and gave us the ministry of reconciliation: ¹⁹ that God was reconciling the world to himself in Christ, not counting men's sins against them. And he has committed to us the message of reconciliation.

Kingly and Priestly Office and Duty

EPHESIANS 2:19

¹⁹ Consequently, you are no longer foreigners and aliens, but fellow citizens with God's people and members of God's household,

ROMANS 15:14–16

[14] I myself am convinced, my brothers, that you yourselves are full of goodness, complete in knowledge and competent to instruct one another. [15] I have written you quite boldly on some points, as if to remind you of them again, because of the grace God gave me [16] to be a minister of Christ Jesus to the Gentiles with the priestly duty of proclaiming the gospel of God, so that the Gentiles might become an offering acceptable to God, sanctified by the Holy Spirit.

REVELATION 20:6

[6] Blessed and holy are those who have part in the first resurrection. The second death has no power over them, but they will be priests of God and of Christ and will reign with him for a thousand years.

QUESTIONS FOR REVIEW

1. In your observation, can you identify some of the outstanding problems with Christianity? Please explain.

_____
_____
_____

2. What is the essence of the New Covenant ministry?

_____
_____
_____

3. Who is the main "actor" in the New Covenant ministry? How so?

_____
_____
_____

4. Give a brief observation of the relationship between the Kingdom of God and the Household of God.

QUESTIONS
FOR MEDITATION & APPLICATION

1. What is your idea of being a minister? How are you to become a New Covenant minister?

_____

_____

_____

2. How do you think you can practically serve the Lord in the place where God has you?

_____

_____

_____

3. What do kingly and priestly duties mean to you? Do you think there are only heavenly things? If not, why?

_____

_____

4. How do you think you can attain a deeper level of God's wisdom? For what?

12

THE BODY OF CHRIST AND OUR ROLES IN IT

OVERVIEW

This chapter will give a brief review of our life in Christ, individually as well as corporately. We will use different analogies in the Bible to paint a broad picture of the Body of Christ and our roles in it:

- The Corporate Man of Christ

- The Body of Christ and Its Many Members

- The Bride of Christ and Her Marriage

- The Church of Christ and Its Priests

- The Temple of God and Its Precious Stones

- The Family of God and Its Many Sons

The Body of Christ is a spiritual organism that evolves much like a natural life, but it is also a living entity that functions like an institution or a kingdom. It exists and progresses in Heaven, or the heavenly realms. At the same time, it is planted and fostered in a society and culture on earth. Therefore, it inevitably takes on certain characteristics as a social entity like a family, a community, an institution, even a nation—a conglomerate of the people of God in various settings and generations.

In the Bible, many analogies are used to describe its nature and functions, its constitution and institution, its life and economy. Please keep in mind that in this chapter we will not discuss the Kingdom of God and its government in the context of a spiritual conflict between the Kingdom of Light and the Kingdom of Darkness, which is essential and necessary, but let's reserve this topic for another time. Rather, we will concentrate more on the context of spiritual life as the corporate Body of Christ—the Family and Household of God.

THE CORPORATE MAN OF CHRIST

Before He created the world, God the Father had in His mind that He would have a family of sons, even a kingdom of priests. This plan was "disrupted" because of man's disobedience. Even so, through Christ, He is reconciling man (Adam) and everything else back to Himself to fulfill His full intention for mankind and all creation.

In this corporate Man, the image (birthright—position and

honor) and the likeness (embodiment—life and expression) of the Spirit of sonship, is destined to be perfected (or come to its fullness) in and through Christ Jesus as its Head, and through those who believe in him as its Body. This is the greatest and the ultimate mystery of God, of heaven and earth, of men and angels. It had been hidden throughout all the ages until Jesus came and taught about it. Yet even his disciples could not fully grasp its essence, its grace, and its power even after they were sent to preach the Kingdom of God. For example, Peter had a hard time accepting the fact that the Gentiles were also included in God's promise, and in Christ. In God, they would be regarded as the same as the Jews, even as one people (Acts 10). It was to Paul that this great mystery was fully revealed, and with it, the administration of it. Paul was called to bring the gospel to the Gentiles. Like Peter, Paul also had to wait for many years for this revelation to mature and saturate in his own heart.

Let's look at this in the scriptures:

EPHESIANS 2:13-18
[13] But now in Christ Jesus you who once were far away have been brought near through the blood of Christ.
[14] For he himself is our peace, who has made the two one and has destroyed the barrier, the dividing wall of hostility, [15] by abolishing in his flesh the law with its commandments and regulations. His purpose was to create in himself one new man out of the two, thus making peace, [16] and in this one body to reconcile both of them to God through the cross, by which he put to death their hostility. [17] He came and preached peace to you who were far away and peace to those who were near. [18] For through him we both have access to the Father by one Spirit.

EPHESIANS 3:1-12

¹ For this reason I, Paul, the prisoner of Christ Jesus for the sake of you Gentiles— ² Surely you have heard about the administration of God's grace that was given to me for you, ³ that is, the mystery made known to me by revelation, as I have already written briefly.

⁴ In reading this, then, you will be able to understand my insight into the mystery of Christ, ⁵ which was not made known to men in other generations as it has now been revealed by the Spirit to God's holy apostles and prophets. ⁶ This mystery is that through the gospel the Gentiles are heirs together with Israel, members together of one body, and sharers together in the promise in Christ Jesus.

⁷ I became a servant of this gospel by the gift of God's grace given me through the working of his power. ⁸ Although I am less than the least of all God's people, this grace was given me: to preach to the Gentiles the unsearchable riches of Christ, ⁹ and to make plain to everyone the administration of this mystery, which for ages past was kept hidden in God, who created all things. ¹⁰ His intent was that now, through the church, the manifold wisdom of God should be made known to the rulers and authorities in the heavenly realms, ¹¹ according to his eternal purpose which he accomplished in Christ Jesus our Lord. ¹² In him and through faith in him we may approach God with freedom and confidence.

GALATIANS 2:1-10

¹ Fourteen years later I went up again to Jerusalem, this time with Barnabas. I took Titus along also. ² I went in response to a revelation and set before them the gospel that I preach among the Gentiles. But I did this privately to those who seemed to be leaders, for fear that I was running or had run my race in vain. ³ Yet not even Titus, who was with me, was compelled to be circumcised, even though he was a Greek. ⁴ This matter arose because some false brothers had infiltrated our ranks to spy on the freedom we have in

Christ Jesus and to make us slaves. ⁵ *We did not give into them for a moment, so that the truth of the gospel might remain with you.* ⁶ *As for those who seemed to be important—whatever they were makes no difference to me; God does not judge by external appearance—those men added nothing to my message.* ⁷ *On the contrary, they saw that I had been entrusted with the task of preaching the gospel to the Gentiles, just as Peter had been to the Jews.* ⁸ *For God, who was at work in the ministry of Peter as an apostle to the Jews, was also at work in my ministry as an apostle to the Gentiles.* ⁹ *James, Peter and John, those reputed to be pillars, gave me and Barnabas the right hand of fellowship when they recognized the grace given to me. They agreed that we should go to the Gentiles, and they to the Jews.* ¹⁰ *All they asked was that we should continue to remember the poor, the very thing I was eager to do.*

THE BODY OF CHRIST AND ITS MEMBERS

In essence, every believer of Christ is brought into this New Man, the last Adam, through whom sin and death is cancelled, and our alienation from God the Father is no more. We become the Body of Christ, or the corporate Man of Christ, of which Jesus is the Head and we are its many members.

In a human body, the head governs all the other parts. All parts or members work together as a whole. It would be unthinkable to tell the head not to order the members around, or to have each member doing its own thing when a move or a task is to be carried out. To pick up a book, we need to think about it with the mind, locate it with our eyes, and then use our hands to do it. However, even the hands cannot function apart from the arms, nor the arms without the shoulders and so on. Each part must function in perfect unity with the will or command of the head. These actions have become so routine and natural in our lives, that we do not marvel at them at all. Yet the principles and mechanisms behind such simple actions are incredibly intriguing, and cannot be fully replicated by any other form of life or reproduced by any human design.

In the Body of Christ, the Holy Spirit is like the head and the nervous system. The Spirit is the coordinator and enabler of all members, the conscious and cognitive part of a spiritual man. Part of this has to do with the coordination and cooperation of our spiritual gifts in a corporate setting. This means that our personal gifts and roles are to be appropriated by the head and used for the benefit of the whole body. The eye, hand, arm, and shoulder work together to fulfill the task designated by the head in the above example.

Let's look at this in the scriptures:

ROMANS 12:4-8
⁴ Just as each of us has one body with many members, and these members do not all have the same function, ⁵ so in Christ we who are many form one body, and each member belongs to all the others. ⁶ We have different gifts, according to the grace given us. If a man's gift is prophesying, let him use it in proportion to his faith. ⁷ If it is serving, let him serve; if it is teaching, let him teach; ⁸ if it is encouraging, let him encourage; if it is contributing to the needs of others, let him give generously; if it is leadership, let him govern diligently; if it is showing mercy, let him do it cheerfully.

In the natural, it takes a process of maturity for a human body to come to its full stature. As it matures, members of the body will learn to cope with different tasks with increasing capacity and harmony. Maturity of a spiritual body can be quite different in terms of the realities and agents involved, but the similarity of the process between the two is obvious.

> **EPHESIANS 4:11–16**
> *[11] It was he who gave some to be apostles, some to be prophets, some to be evangelists, and some to be pastors and teachers, [12] to prepare God's people for works of service, so that the body of Christ may be built up [13] until we all reach unity in the faith and in the knowledge of the Son of God and become mature, attaining to the whole measure of the fullness of Christ.*
> *[14] Then we will no longer be infants, tossed back and forth by the waves, and blown here and there by every wind of teaching and by the cunning and craftiness of men in their deceitful scheming.*
> *[15] Instead, speaking the truth in love, we will in all things grow up into him who is the Head, that is, Christ. [16] From him the whole body, joined and held together by every supporting ligament, grows and builds itself up in love, as each part does its work.*

THE BRIDE OF CHRIST AND HER MARRIAGE

Again, the concept and practice of marriage in the natural did not begin with Jesus Christ, the last Adam, but with the first Adam.

Recorded in Genesis 2, when God saw that Adam had no suitable companion, he said: "It is not good for the man to be alone. I will make a helper suitable for him." He took a bone from Adam's rib, and from it made the woman as his helper.

> **GENESIS 2:23-24**
> *[23] The man said,*
> *"This is now bone of my bones and flesh of my flesh; she shall be called 'woman,' for she was taken out of man."*
> *[24] For this reason a man will leave his father and mother and be united to his wife, and they will become one flesh.*

Hidden here is the mystery of Christ and His Bride. The father will prepare a bride for the son and is in great anticipation of their wedding feast. In one light, as members of the Church of Christ Jesus, we are one spiritual body or one flesh with him who is the Head. In another, we are the Bride (virgin daughter of Zion or virgin Jerusalem), or the woman, made by the Father as a suitable helper (partner) for the Son.

Jesus mentioned this on numerous occasions in the scriptures. Let's look at one:

> **MATTHEW 22:1-4**
> *[1] Jesus spoke to them again in parables, saying: [2] "The kingdom of heaven is like a king who prepared a wedding banquet for his son.*
> *[3] He sent his servants to those who had been invited to the banquet to tell them to come, but they refused to come.*
> *[4] "Then he sent some more servants and said, 'Tell those who have been invited that I have prepared my dinner: My oxen and fattened cattle have been butchered, and everything is ready. Come to the wedding banquet.'*

Here the wedding is for the Son and his Bride. The servants of God are to betroth others to Christ as they become his disciples, as mentioned by John the Baptist and the apostle Paul.

JOHN 3:25–30

²⁵ An argument developed between some of John's disciples and a certain Jew over the matter of ceremonial washing. ²⁶ They came to John and said to him, "Rabbi, that man who was with you on the other side of the Jordan—the one you testified about—well, he is baptizing, and everyone is going to him."
²⁷ To this John replied, "A man can receive only what is given him from heaven. ²⁸ You yourselves can testify that I said, 'I am not the Christ but am sent ahead of him.' ²⁹ The bride belongs to the bridegroom. The friend who attends the bridegroom waits and listens for him, and is full of joy when he hears the bridegroom's voice. That joy is mine, and it is now complete. ³⁰ He must become greater; I must become less.

2 CORINTHIANS 11:2–5

² I am jealous for you with a godly jealousy. I promised you to one husband, to Christ, so that I might present you as a pure virgin to him. ³ But I am afraid that just as Eve was deceived by the serpent's cunning, your minds may somehow be led astray from your sincere and pure devotion to Christ. ⁴ For if someone comes to you and preaches a Jesus other than the Jesus we preached, or if you receive a different spirit from the one you received, or a different gospel from the one you accepted, you put up with it easily enough.
⁵ But I do not think I am in the least inferior to those "super-apostles."

Paul expounded on this in Ephesians when addressing the issue of the husband and wife relationship.

EPHESIANS 5:25–32
[25] Husbands, love your wives, just as Christ loved the church and gave himself up for her [26] to make her holy, cleansing her by the washing with water through the word, [27] and to present her to himself as a radiant church, without stain or wrinkle or any other blemish, but holy and blameless. [28] In this same way, husbands ought to love their wives as their own bodies. He who loves his wife loves himself. [29] Afterall, no one ever hated his own body, but he feeds and cares for it, just as Christ does the church— [30] for we are members of his body. [31] "For this reason a man will leave his father and mother and be united to his wife, and the two will become one flesh." [32] This is a profound mystery—but I am talking about Christ and the church.

Now, when a man and woman get married, they enter into a covenant with one another as husband and wife. In Jewish tradition, this takes at least two major steps, betrothal and marriage. After a virgin is betrothed to a man, she enters into a process of preparation for marriage. This picture is a shadow of what God the Father is doing with us as the Bride of Christ.

When we become part of his Body through our faith in Christ Jesus, we are then set apart for this divine union. A work of sanctification or purification unto us as his Bride is then carried out by the Holy Spirit on the Father's behalf. That is the teaching of the Word of God, which sanctifies us to become blameless and spotless before God. "The one who is holy" now makes us holy unto God (Hebrews 2:11).

THE CHURCH OF CHRIST AND ITS PRIESTS

This holiness was implied when Jesus designated his believers as the Church.

> **MATTHEW 16:18–19**
> *¹⁸ And I tell you that you are Peter, and on this rock I will build my church, and the gates of Hades will not overcome it. ¹⁹ I will give you the keys of the kingdom of heaven; whatever you bind on earth will be bound in heaven, and whatever you loose on earth will be loosed in heaven."*

Let's look at the word "church." It comes from the Greek word "ekklesia",

> "From ek, out of, and klēsis, a calling (kaleō, to call), was used among the Greeks of a body of citizens gathered to discuss the affairs of state."[f]

In the above teaching, Jesus is obviously talking about his Church as a spiritual entity that is entrusted with the power to overthrow the Kingdom of Darkness. Paul expounds on this here:

> **EPHESIANS 3:10–11**
> *¹⁰ His intent was that now, through the church, the manifold wisdom*

---

[f] Vine, W.E. *Vine's Complete Expository Dictionary of Old and New Testament Words.* Thomas Nelson, 1984.

of God should be made known to the rulers and authorities in the heavenly realms, ¹¹ according to his eternal purpose which he accomplished in Christ Jesus our Lord.

Notice that as a spiritual entity, the Church is made up of many members as a spiritual people or nation, and it does not exist without order and ranks—as many presume to think. The apostles John and Paul (like Jacob, Moses, David, Isaac, and other prophets of old) were caught up into heaven and given revelations of this gathering or assembly of God's people as expounded on in the book of Hebrews, in Revelation 21, and in many other scriptures.

Let's read a key portion:

HEBREWS 12:22-24
²² But you have come to Mount Zion, to the heavenly Jerusalem, the city of the living God. You have come to thousands upon thousands of angels in joyful assembly, ²³ to the church of the firstborn, whose names are written in heaven. You have come to God, the judge of all men, to the spirits of righteous men made perfect, ²⁴ to Jesus the mediator of a new covenant, and to the sprinkled blood that speaks a better word than the blood of Abel.

There is another instance where Jesus mentioned the concept of the Church. He used it to denote a community or assembly of believers here on earth. Let's take a look.

MATTHEW 18:17-18
¹⁷ If he refuses to listen to them, tell it to the church; and if he refuses to listen even to the church, treat him as you would a pagan

or a tax collector.
¹⁸ "I tell you the truth, whatever you bind on earth will be bound in heaven, and whatever you loose on earth will be loosed in heaven.

However, even here the Church is not portrayed as merely an earthly social or religious entity. Jesus clearly entrusted such a group of people with his heavenly authority and power. It is rather a chosen or elected leadership amongst the believers of Jesus Christ who are "spiritually appraised" and officially designated through the work of the Holy Spirit according to a heavenly order. Paul expounds on this with more detail:

EPHESIANS 4:4–13
⁴ There is one body and one Spirit—just as you were called to one hope when you were called— ⁵ one Lord, one faith, one baptism; ⁶ one God and Father of all, who is over all and through all and in all.
⁷ But to each one of us grace has been given as Christ apportioned it.
⁸ This is why it says:
"When he ascended on high, he led captives in his train and gave gifts to men."
⁹ (What does "he ascended" mean except that he also descended to the lower, earthly regions? ¹⁰ He who descended is the very one who ascended higher than all the heavens, in order to fill the whole universe.) ¹¹ It was he who gave some to be apostles, some to be prophets, some to be evangelists, and some to be pastors and teachers, ¹² to prepare God's people for works of service, so that the body of Christ may be built up ¹³ until we all reach unity in the faith and in the knowledge of the Son of God and become mature, attaining to the whole measure of the fullness of Christ.

The governing order that Jesus laid out for the Church is to be appropriated in a community or a family setting. In many ways, it is similar to the Jewish synagogue and its local community of the day. However, the cultural and religious practices of the Church as a spiritual entity and people are fundamentally different from the practices of the Jews. It is not regulated by a law of dos and don'ts, like the law of Moses. Rather, it is the order of spiritual worship and service in the spiritual temple of God, "on earth as it is in heaven." Those of the Church are an order of spiritual worship or service in His heavenly tabernacle, on earth as it is in heaven. Here lies the mystery of the pattern and practice of the oneness of God in the Holy Spirit. The Church is the living expression of God on earth and in heaven as the Body of Christ. It is one with the Son (Jesus Christ, being its Head) as a spiritual Body or union, and one with the Father, being the exact representation and reflection of God, perfect in every way as His image and likeness. It is the expressed life and glory of God. Paul explains it in this way:

> **"The Church is the living expression of God on earth and in heaven as the Body of Christ."**

COLOSSIANS 2:1-10

¹ I want you to know how much I am struggling for you and for those at Laodicea, and for all who have not met me personally. ² My purpose is that they may be encouraged in heart and united in love, so that they may have the full riches of complete understanding, in order that they may know the mystery of God, namely, Christ, ³ in whom are hidden all the treasures of wisdom and knowledge. ⁴ *I tell you this so that no one may deceive you by fine-sounding arguments.* ⁵ *For though I am absent from you in body, I am present with you in spirit and delight to see how orderly you are and how firm your faith in Christ is.*

⁶ *So then, just as you received Christ Jesus as Lord, continue to live in him,* ⁷ *rooted and built up in him, strengthened in the faith as you were taught, and overflowing with thankfulness.*
⁸ *See to it that no one takes you captive through hollow and deceptive philosophy, which depends on human tradition and the basic principles of this world rather than on Christ.*
⁹ *For in Christ all the fullness of the Deity lives in bodily form,*
¹⁰ *and you have been given fullness in Christ, who is the head over every power and authority.*

In summary, the Church means a people that are called out from the normal social, political, cultural, or religious contexts to be set apart as holy unto God, so that they can worship God the Father in spirit and in truth, as citizens of the Kingdom of Jesus Christ and members of His Family.

A side note:
This is exactly the calling God had for the Israelites when He delivered them out of Egypt. God's intent was that they would be a people set part for Himself to show His glory and His holiness unto all people of the world, to be a kingdom of priests for Him.

EXODUS 19:1–6
¹ *In the third month after the Israelites left Egypt—on the very day—they came to the Desert of Sinai.* ² *After they set out from*

Rephidim, they entered the Desert of Sinai, and Israel camped there in the desert in front of the mountain.
³ Then Moses went up to God, and the Lord called to him from the mountain and said, "This is what you are to say to the house of Jacob and what you are to tell the people of Israel: ⁴ 'You yourselves have seen what I did to Egypt, and how I carried you on eagles' wings and brought you to myself. ⁵ Now if you obey me fully and keep my covenant, then out of all nations you will be my treasured possession. Although the whole earth is mine, ⁶ you will be for me a kingdom of priests and a holy nation.' These are the words you are to speak to the Israelites."

THE TEMPLE OF GOD AND ITS PRECIOUS STONES

Before Jesus Christ came, all of man's endeavors to attain true godliness had miserably failed. For it is never a work that could be accomplished by human strength. No, it is solely reserved for the spirit of the Father working with the spirit of the Son, as prophesied by Zechariah:

ZECHARIAH 4:6–10
⁶ So he said to me, "This is the word of the Lord to Zerubbabel: 'Not by might nor by power, but by my Spirit,' says the Lord Almighty.
⁷ "What are you, O mighty mountain? Before Zerubbabel you will become level ground. Then he will bring out the capstone to shouts of 'God bless it! God bless it!'"
⁸ Then the word of the Lord came to me:
⁹ "The hands of Zerubbabel have laid the foundation of this temple; his hands will also complete it. Then you will know that the

Lord Almighty has sent me to you.
¹⁰ "Who dares despise the day of small things, since the seven eyes of the Lord that range throughout the earth will rejoice when they see the chosen capstone in the hand of Zerubbabel?"

Here, God uses the pattern for the new temple (the latter house as mentioned in Haggai 2) to symbolize the work that is to be accomplished by the Church.

Now again let's read Jesus' own words.

MATTHEW 16:18–19
¹⁸ And I tell you that you are Peter, and on this rock I will build my church, and the gates of Hades will not overcome it. ¹⁹ I will give you the keys of the kingdom of heaven; whatever you bind on earth will be bound in heaven, and whatever you loose on earth will be loosed in heaven."

In this context, it is clear that the concept and actualization of sonship (the Messiah, or Christ, the Anointed One) is the rock upon which the Church is to be built. This Truth is called the cornerstone (Isaiah 28:16), which is Christ. He is the foundation or bedrock of our spiritual life (1 Corinthians 3:11). He is also the capstone (Psalm 118:22) and the plumb line, which is righteousness and justice (Isaiah 28:17). This concept is mentioned many times by the apostles Paul, Peter, and others. Let's look.

1 CORINTHIANS 3:9–11
⁹ For we are God's fellow workers; you are God's field, God's building.
¹⁰ By the grace God has given me, I laid a foundation as an expert

builder, and someone else is building on it. But each one should be careful how he builds. ¹¹ For no one can lay any foundation other than the one already laid, which is Jesus Christ.

EPHESIANS 2:19-22

¹⁹ Consequently, you are no longer foreigners and aliens, but fellow citizens with God's people and members of God's household, ²⁰built on the foundation of the apostles and prophets, with Christ Jesus himself as the chief cornerstone. ²¹ In him the whole building is joined together and rises to become a holy temple in the Lord. ²² And in him you too are being built together to become a dwelling in which God lives by his Spirit.

1 PETER 2:4-10

⁴ As you come to him, the living Stone—rejected by men but chosen by God and precious to him— ⁵ you also, like living stones, are being built into a spiritual house to be a holy priesthood, offering spiritual sacrifices acceptable to God through Jesus Christ. ⁶ For in Scripture it says:

"See, I lay a stone in Zion, a chosen and precious cornerstone, and the one who trusts in him will never be put to shame."

⁷ Now to you who believe, this stone is precious. But to those who do not believe,

"The stone the builders rejected has become the capstone,"

⁸ and,

"A stone that causes men to stumble and a rock that makes them fall."

They stumble because they disobey the message—which is also what they were destined for.

⁹ But you are a chosen people, a royal priesthood, a holy nation, a people belonging to God, that you may declare the praises of him who called you out of darkness into his wonderful light. ¹⁰ Once you were not a people, but now you are the people of God; once you had not received mercy, but now you have received mercy.

THE FAMILY OF GOD AND ITS MANY SONS

Now, we are the people of God, belonging to His Household, which is the Family of God. We are no longer excluded from any of His promises to mankind. Through Christ Jesus, all of them are fulfilled.

2 CORINTHIANS 1:20-22
[20] For no matter how many promises God has made, they are "Yes" in Christ. And so through him the "Amen" is spoken by us to the glory of God. [21] Now it is God who makes both us and you stand firm in Christ. He anointed us, [22] set his seal of ownership on us, and put his Spirit in our hearts as a deposit, guaranteeing what is to come.

Ultimately, the eternal covenant of the Father and the Son is fulfilled or perfected in and through us as the Body of Christ. We are in him and he in us, and through us he will accomplish what God the Father had purposed from the beginning.

EPHESIANS 1:4-10
[4] For he chose us in him before the creation of the world to be holy and blameless in his sight. In love [5] he predestined us to be adopted as his sons through Jesus Christ, in accordance with his pleasure and will— [6] to the praise of his glorious grace, which he has freely given us in the One he loves. [7] In him we have redemption through his blood, the forgiveness of sins, in accordance with the

riches of God's grace ⁸ that he lavished on us with all wisdom and understanding. ⁹ And he made known to us the mystery of his will according to his good pleasure, which he purposed in Christ, ¹⁰ to be put into effect when the times will have reached their fulfillment—to bring all
things in heaven and on earth together under one head, even Christ.

Now, for this reason God gave us the Spirit of sonship as mentioned by John.

JOHN 1:12–13
¹² Yet to all who received him, to those who believed in his name, he gave the right to become children of God— ¹³ children born not of natural descent, nor of human decision or a husband's will, but born of God.

Now, if we are God's sons, then we are also His heirs and share the Father's inheritance with Christ Jesus.

ROMANS 8:16–17
¹⁶ The Spirit himself testifies with our spirit that we are God's children. ¹⁷ Now if we are children, then we are heirs—heirs of God and co-heirs with Christ, if indeed we share in his sufferings in order that we may also share in his glory.

As in any case, we will not only enjoy the benefit of our family, but we will also share in the responsibility. It is our hope that, through this series of teachings, we have assisted you in your noble quest as a son of God, a citizen of the Kingdom of Christ, and a member of God's family.

SCRIPTURES

GENESIS 3:16

¹⁶ *To the woman he said, "I will greatly increase your pains in childbearing; with pain you will give birth to children. Your desire will be for your husband, and he will rule over you."*

PSALM 45:10–17

¹⁰ *Listen, O daughter, consider and give ear:*
Forget your people and your father's house.
¹¹ *The king is enthralled by your beauty;*
honor him, for he is your lord.
¹² *The Daughter of Tyre will come with a gift,*
men of wealth will seek your favor.
¹³ *All glorious is the princess within her chamber;*
her gown is interwoven with gold.
¹⁴ *In embroidered garments she is led to the king;*
her virgin companions follow her
and are brought to you.
¹⁵ *They are led in with joy and gladness;*
they enter the palace of the king.
¹⁶ *Your sons will take the place of your fathers;*
you will make them princes throughout the land.
¹⁷ *I will perpetuate your memory through all generations;*
therefore the nations will praise you for ever and ever.

HAGGAI 2:7–9

⁷ *I will shake all nations, and the desired of all nations will come, and I will fill this house with glory,' says the Lord Almighty.* ⁸ *'The silver is mine and the gold is mine,' declares the Lord Almighty.* ⁹ *'The glory of this present house will be greater than the glory of the former house,' says*

the Lord Almighty. 'And in this place I will grant peace,' declares the Lord Almighty.'"

REVELATION 21:9–10

⁹ One of the seven angels who had the seven bowls full of the seven last plagues came and said to me, "Come, I will show you the bride, the wife of the Lamb." ¹⁰ And he carried me away in the Spirit to a mountain great and high, and showed me the Holy City, Jerusalem, coming down out of heaven from God.

MATTHEW 10:32–40

³² "Whoever acknowledges me before men, I will also acknowledge him before my Father in heaven. ³³ But whoever disowns me before men, I will disown him before my Father in heaven.
³⁴ "Do not suppose that I have come to bring peace to the earth. I did not come to bring peace, but a sword. ³⁵ For I have come to turn
"'a man against his father, a daughter against her mother, a daughter-in-law against her mother-in-law— ³⁶ a man's enemies will be the members of his own household.'
³⁷ Anyone who loves his father or mother more than me is not worthy of me; anyone who loves his son or daughter more than me is not worthy of me; ³⁸ and anyone who does not take his cross and follow me is not worthy of me. ³⁹ Whoever finds his life will lose it, and whoever loses his life for my sake will find it.
⁴⁰ "He who receives you receives me, and he who receives me receives the one who sent me.

1 CORINTHIANS 12:12–28

¹² The body is a unit, though it is made up of many parts; and though all its parts are many, they form one body. So it is with Christ. ¹³ For we were all baptized by one Spirit into one body—whether Jews or Greeks, slave or free—and we were all given the one Spirit to drink. ¹⁴ Now the

body is not made up of one part but of many.
¹⁵ If the foot should say, "Because I am not a hand, I do not belong to the body," it would not for that reason cease to be part of the body.
¹⁶ And if the ear should say, "Because I am not an eye, I do not belong to the body," it would not for that reason cease to be part of the body.
¹⁷ If the whole body were an eye, where would the sense of hearing be? If the whole body were an ear, where would the sense of smell be? ¹⁸ But in fact God has arranged the parts in the body, every one of them, just as he wanted them to be. ¹⁹ If they were all one part, where would the body be? ²⁰ As it is, there are many parts, but one body.
²¹ The eye cannot say to the hand, "I don't need you!" And the head cannot say to the feet, "I don't need you!" ²² On the contrary, those parts of the body that seem to be weaker are indispensable, ²³ and the parts that we think are less honorable we treat with special honor. And the parts that are unpresentable are treated with special modesty, ²⁴ while our presentable parts need no special treatment. But God has combined the members of the body and has given greater honor to the parts that lacked it, ²⁵ so that there should be no division in the body, but that its parts should have equal concern for each other. ²⁶ If one part suffers, every part suffers with it; if one part is honored, every part rejoices with it.
²⁷ Now you are the body of Christ, and each one of you is a part of it. ²⁸ And in the church God has appointed first of all apostles, second prophets, third teachers, then workers of miracles, also those having gifts of healing, those able to help others, those with gifts of administration, and those speaking in different kinds of tongues.

QUESTIONS FOR REVIEW

1. Review the idea of Man (the purpose for which man was created) from the former chapters. Please explain how and why we are in the Man of Christ as a believer.

_____

_____

_____

2. What do you think the concept of marriage illustrates for us, as we consider our role as the Bride of Christ?

_____

_____

_____

3. How does one become a member of Christ's Body?

_____

_____

4. What does it mean to be a living stone in the Temple or House of God?

5. After having received the Spirit of sonship, do you think we automatically become a mature Son in the Family of God? Why or why not?

QUESTIONS
FOR MEDITATION & APPLICATION

1. What is your role in the Corporate Body of Christ? What has changed since the moment you received Jesus Christ as your Lord and Savior?

_____

_____

_____

2. The Church is a spiritual as well as a social entity. What does that mean to you in your spiritual walk and relationships with others?

_____

_____

_____

3. How do you think you should relate to the Body of Christ in terms of using your gifts, and growing into the fullness of Christ?

_____

Please read these scriptures in Hebrews and answer the following question:

HEBREWS 10:25
²⁵ *Let us not give up meeting together, as some are in the habit of doing, but let us encourage one another—and all the more as you see the Day approaching.*

HEBREWS 12:22–24
²² *But you have come to Mount Zion, to the heavenly Jerusalem, the city of the living God. You have come to thousands upon thousands of angels in joyful assembly,* ²³ *to the church of the firstborn, whose names are written in heaven. You have come to God, the judge of all men, to the spirits of righteous men made perfect,* ²⁴ *to Jesus the mediator of a new covenant, and to the sprinkled blood that speaks a better word than the blood of Abel.*

4. What is the difference between being a member of a local gathering and being a part of the Church in the Heavenly place? What does that mean to you?

APPENDIX A

The information included in this appendix is from *Theological Wordbook of the Old Testament* and has been added for further clarification of this topic.

"Finally, we note two important passages in which man is said to be created in "(the image and) likeness of God" (Genesis 1:26; 5:1), and one passage where Adam fathered a son, Seth, "in his likeness" (Genesis 5:3).

Our purpose here is not to examine per se the doctrine of imago Dei. The studies on this have been numerous. Specifically, we will attempt to ascertain the relationship between selem ("image," q.v.) and dĕmût ("likeness") in Genesis. Nowhere else in the Word do these two nouns appear in parallelism or in connection with each other. The following suggestions have been made.

- Roman Catholic theology has maintained that "image" refers to man's structural likeness to God, a natural image, which survived the Fall and "likeness" refers to man's moral image with which he is supernaturally endowed; and it is this likeness that was destroyed in the Fall.

- The more important word of the two is "image" but to avoid the implication that man is a precise copy of God, albeit in miniature. The less specific and more abstract dĕmût was added. dĕmût then defines and limits the meaning of selem (Humbert, Barr).

- No distinction is to be sought between these two words. They are totally interchangeable. In Genesis 1:26, which is God's resolution to create, both words are used. However, in verse 27 (the actual act of creation) only selem is used, not dĕmût. The two words are so intertwined that nothing is lost in the meaning by the omission of dĕmût. Also, the LXX translates dĕmût in Genesis 5:1 not by the usual homoiosis but by eikon, the Greek counterpart for Hebrew selem in (Schmidt).

- It is not, selem which is defined and limited by (dĕmût) but the other way around. Two things are important here: (a) the similarity between dĕmût and the Hebrew word for "blood" dām; (b) in Mesopotamian tradition the gods in fact created man from divine blood. Genesis then represents a conscious rejection of and polemic against pagan teaching by asserting that selem specifies the divine similarity to which dĕmût refers, viz., man's corporeal appearance and has nothing to do with the blood that flows in his veins (Miller).

- The word "likeness," rather than diminishing the word "image," actually amplifies it and specifies its meaning. Man is not just an image but a likeness—image. He is not simply representative but representational. Man is the visible, corporeal representative of the invisible, bodiless God. Dĕmût guarantees that man is an adequate and faithful representative of God on earth (Clines)."[g]

---

[g] Harris, R. Laird, Gleason L. Archer, and Bruce K. Waltke. *Theological Wordbook of the Old Testament.* Moody, 1981.

TESTIMONIALS

"The teaching within *The Seed* has set the stage in many ways for a radical change in my perspective over the last few years of my life. It is easy when being brought up with a religious or church-based background to assume an understanding of the basic way and move of God. Unfortunately, these assumptions can lead us to a life empty and even robbed of the power of God. *The Seed* is an excellent overview and starting point to recognize the much bigger, much greater way of the Lord. As is implied in the title, the truths presented in *The Seed* do not start or end with the words written here. They come from the ancient way, the true and original way, and set a foundation or starting point into the many wonderful plans that the Lord God has for His people and His Kingdom. It is a great treasure, and has been a mighty blessing in my life."

–Ben L.

"Content expressing pure spiritual truth is hard to find in modern Christianity. Many agendas and perspectives of man have infiltrated modern day teachings about the "truth" of the Gospel, making the real and pure truth about God and his ultimate purpose for mankind unclear and confusing. *The Seed* has been a huge help to me in cutting through the "religious mindsets" of man to get to the pure truth of who God the Father really is, His intent for sending his Son, Jesus Christ, to redeem mankind back to himself, and the ultimate purpose that God has for those who call upon His name. While this process of transformation of my spiritual life is a journey still ongoing that will never stop, *The Seed* series of teachings have been a valuable help to me along the way."

–John C.

"The Lord has established a firm foundation for my relationship with Him through my time with *The Seed* Series. As I receive from Him in this content, my mind is renewed and my spirit resurrected. I consider these teachings an absolute gift from God and a necessity in the season in which we live. I pray His blessings on each of you who seek Him here. Be established! Be enriched! Be empowered! Be released! Be fruitful in the life of sonship in the glorious kingdom of our Father God."

–Cheryl L.

Made in the USA
Middletown, DE
29 October 2022